INVESTING IN DEVELOPING COUNTRIES

**OECD/DAC Member Countries' Policies and
Facilities with Regard to Foreign Direct Investment
in Developing Countries**

**Fifth Revised Edition
November 1982**

ORGANISATION FOR ECONOMIC CO-OPERATION AND DEVELOPMENT

Pursuant to article 1 of the Convention signed in Paris on 14th December, 1960, and which came into force on 30th September, 1961, the Organisation for Economic Co-operation and Development (OECD) shall promote policies designed:

- to achieve the highest sustainable economic growth and employment and a rising standard of living in Member countries, while maintaining financial stability, and thus to contribute to the development of the world economy;
- to contribute to sound economic expansion in Member as well as non-member countries in the process of economic development; and
- to contribute to the expansion of world trade on a multilateral, non-discriminatory basis in accordance with international obligations.

The Signatories of the Convention on the OECD are Austria, Belgium, Canada, Denmark, France, the Federal Republic of Germany, Greece, Iceland, Ireland, Italy, Luxembourg, the Netherlands, Norway, Portugal, Spain, Sweden, Switzerland, Turkey, the United Kingdom and the United States. The following countries acceded subsequently to this Convention (the dates are those on which the instruments of accession were deposited): Japan (28th April, 1964), Finland (28th January, 1969), Australia (7th June, 1971) and New Zealand (29th May, 1973).

The Socialist Federal Republic of Yugoslavia takes part in certain work of the OECD (agreement of 28th October, 1961).

In order to achieve its aims the OECD has set up a number of specialised committees. One of these is the Development Assistance Committee, whose Members have agreed to secure an expansion of aggregate volume of resources made available to developing countries and to improve their effectiveness. To this end, Members periodically review together both the amount and the nature of their contributions to aid programmes, bilateral and multilateral, and consult each other on all other relevant aspects of their development assistance policies.
The Members of the Development Assistance Committee are Australia, Austria, Belgium, Canada, Denmark, Finland, France, the Federal Republic of Germany, Italy, Japan, the Netherlands, New Zealand, Norway, Sweden, Switzerland, the United Kingdom, the United States and the Commission of the European Economic Communities.

Publié en français sous le titre:

INVESTIR DANS LE TIERS MONDE

Cover picture: A generator plant in Germany is filling export orders made possible by investment flows to developing countries. (Courtesy Bundesbild Bonn.)

The first edition of this Survey was published in 1972 under the responsibility of the Secretary-General and has been updated at regular intervals by the Development Co-operation Directorate.

Also available

DEVELOPMENT CO-OPERATION. 1982 REVIEW
(43 82 03 1) ISBN 92-64-12392-X   £9.50   US$19   F95

GEOGRAPHICAL DISTRIBUTION OF FINANCIAL FLOWS TO DEVEL-OPING COUNTRIES 1978-1981
(43 82 02 3) ISBN 92-64-02355-0 Bil.   £11.00   US$22.00   F110.00

EXTERNAL DEBT OF DEVELOPING COUNTRIES. 1982 Survey
(43 83 01 1) ISBN 92-64-12395-4   £6.00   US$12.00   F60.00

CONTENTS

Part I:

List of Tables:

Part I

OVERVIEW

1. THE ROLE OF FOREIGN DIRECT INVESTMENT IN ECONOMIC CO-OPERATION WITH DEVELOPING COUNTRIES

Foreign direct investment constitutes a resource flow which is particularly useful for the economic development of developing countries, especially for their industrial development. It provides a unique combination of long-term finance, technology, training, know-how, managerial expertise and marketing experience. Moreover, the balance of payments cost of direct (equity) investment in the form of profit remittances is a function of the commercial success of the foreign venture rather than occurring as fixed interest payments, as in the case of borrowing. Developing countries seem increasingly to recognise these advantages, and in recent years have witnessed a rapid, though erratic, growth of direct investment flows to them.

While developing countries are increasingly significant recipients of DAC Members' foreign direct investment, the bulk of such investment still flows to other OECD countries: Of new foreign investment flows, more than two-thirds were directed in recent years to other Member countries. At present, direct investment assets held by enterprises from DAC countries in the Third World represent about one quarter of the total world stock of foreign investment originating in DAC Member countries[1].

It is important to emphasize that the choice for an entrepreneur who wants to establish a venture abroad is worldwide and that in a majority of cases, especially for smaller, less experienced enterprises, the decision is

---

1. This ratio varies widely for different countries, as illustrated by the following estimates: Japan 51 per cent, Germany 30 per cent, United Kingdom 24 per cent, United States 21 per cent, Switzerland 9 per cent (see: International Investment and Multinational Enterprises - Recent International Direct Investment Trends, OECD, Paris 1981, Tables 2 and 10.

not in favour of location in the Third World. Developing countries therefore have to compete with other host countries in attracting foreign direct investment. Experience has shown that measures undertaken by home and host governments to improve the flow of foreign direct investment or to direct it to specific sectors and locations influence investment decisions only marginally. Such incentives can never substitute for the "fundamentals": the investment climate, political security and profit opportunities.

In competing with industrialised countries for foreign direct investment, developing countries can often offer a number of genuine comparative advantages: natural resources, low-cost labour, local and export markets, a relatively less powerful focus on social and environmental objectives, and lower taxes. These advantages, however, are sometimes outweighed by negative factors of an economic, political or even psychological character: lack of supportive infrastructure, lack of skilled labour, incohesive development policy, political risk and uncertainties surrounding the decision-making process. On balance, developing countries which have successfully attracted direct investment from the OECD area are mainly those with a dynamic and outward looking economic stance sustained by appropriate financial and economic policies, a disciplined labour force and, at the time of transaction, a good international credit standing. Examples of such countries include the European developing countries and some other newly-industrialising countries (NICs) which, at an early stage, decided to adopt liberal economic policies and to integrate their economies into the world economy. Over half of new investment from DAC countries in developing countries in recent years was directed to these countries.

Such a propitious general economic environment is particularly attractive if accompanied by clear and stable investment conditions, and the ability to generate a large range of productive investment projects. Stability of investment conditions, non-discrimination ("national treatment"), freedom of capital movements, and satisfactory arrangements for the settlement of investment disputes are features of investment security to which foreign investors attach particular importance.

By its very nature (and in contrast to most other external resources) foreign investment involves some foreign control over the host country's internal economic activity. This remains the cause of some of the tension over foreign direct investment in North-South relations. Each developing country is, of course, free in its sovereign decision to accept or to reject foreign direct investment or to limit it to certain sectors and economic activities. It is important, however, that those developing countries which have chosen to use foreign

8

direct investment as an instrument of development should create and maintain mutually beneficial investment conditions. The conditions have to meet the need both to secure adequate benefits for the host country and take account of the legitimate interests of foreign investors.

2. FOREIGN DIRECT INVESTMENT ISSUES IN INTERNATIONAL DISCUSSIONS

During the 1960s and 1970s, the role of foreign direct investment in the development of Third World host countries has been an issue of intense discussion in various international fora. In 1967 the OECD adopted a Draft Convention on the Protection of Foreign Property, stating principles of international law applicable in this area. Though never ratified, this Convention has since served as a model for a great and increasing number of bilateral investment promotion and protection treaties between industrialised and developing countries. The International Chamber of Commerce (which includes many developing countries), through its Guidelines for International Investment of 1972, addressed "practical recommendations" to foreign investors as well as to their home and host countries.

In 1976, OECD Member countries agreed on a Declaration and Decisions on Guidelines for Multinational Enterprises (revised in 1979). They deal with Guidelines for Multinational Enterprises, national treatment for firms under foreign control, incentives and disincentives for international investment, and consultation procedures. Though primarily concerned with intra-OECD foreign direct investments, this work has also had, and will continue to have, implications for Member countries' positions on foreign direct investment in developing countries.

The Conference on International Economic Cooperation (CIEC), convened in 1976 after the first oil price shock, discussed, among other things, the contribution of foreign direct investment to the development process. In its final report of June 1977, the Conference stressed the important role of foreign investment for economic development. It stated a number of conditions, agreed upon by Conference participants, for enhancing this role and increasing the flow of foreign direct investment, in particular a satisfactory investment climate. No agreement was reached, however, concerning compensation in case of expropriation, repatriation of profits and capital, and procedures for the settlement of investment disputes. It is interesting to note that, at the Conference, oil-exporting developing countries were already demanding protection of their assets in OECD countries against inflation and currency depreciation, restrictions on capital movements, taxation, political risks and coercive measures (confiscation, freezing, conversion and transfer restrictions). It was not possible to reach agreement on these requests which would have meant special treatment of a certain category of foreign investors.

In 1979, the Conference of the International Labour Organisation adopted a "Tripartite Declaration of Principles concerning Multinational Enterprises and Social Policy". A Code on Restrictive Business Practices was adopted by the UN General Assembly in 1980; negotiations in UNCTAD on an International Code of Conduct on the Transfer of Technology are still continuing, whereas discussions in the UN on an International Agreement on Illicit Payments broke down in 1980.

The UN Commission on Transnational Corporations, established in 1974 by the ECOSOC, and its Intergovernmental Working Group on a Code of Conduct, are designing a set of rules acceptable to all parties concerned with foreign investment. Drafts of a "Code of Conduct for Transnational Corporations" have been discussed for quite some time, with active participation of Member countries of the OECD Committee on International Investment and Multinational Enterprises. Major political and legal difficulties remain to be solved, however, before a draft Code can be presented to the UN General Assembly.

A Task Force on Private Foreign Investment, established in 1978 by the IMF/IBRD Development Committee, has submitted a report on its findings in August 1980. The report concludes inter alia:

"Increasing flows of private foreign direct investment to developing nations is especially important at the present time, given the difficulties many are having in adjusting to growing balance of payments deficits. The Task Force noted the increasing use of new forms of investment, some of which comprise aspects other than ownership and involve less control by the investor over the activities generated."

"The Task Force recommends that home countries eliminate disincentives to investment abroad, and provide some incentives to private investment in developing countries."

"The Task Force examined two major categories of host country policies: incentives to foreign investment and performance requirements. Host countries' use of such measures is oriented toward allocating direct foreign investment in accordance with national objectives and priorities. However, in some cases the use of such measures may work to their disadvantage. Recognising that the impact of foreign investment incentives is not known with certainty, and may in any event not be a major factor in the decisions of foreign investors, sometimes they may represent a needless expenditure of resources, while at other times they may increase the net benefits for recipient countries. Performance requirements may also, under certain circumstances, discourage investment or produce distortions in the economy of the host country. In view of the present lack of information concerning the precise impact of both incentives and performance requirements, a first step should be to study and analyse existing foreign investment incentives and performance requirements and to consider how their quantitative and qualitative impact can be assessed." The task of carrying out such a study has been assigned to the IFC.

The OECD Committee on International Investment and Multinational Enterprises (CIME), which has an overall co-ordinating function for OECD activities in the foreign direct investment area, also started to discuss problems concerning foreign direct investment in developing countries(2).

Finally, the OECD Development Centre is studying several aspects of foreign investment and their impact on development, with particular emphasis on new forms of investment, international banking and financial markets in developing countries, and the role of export processing zones. The first results of this programme, which was carried out by research teams of selected developing and developed countries, are already available(3).

3. OFFICIAL MEASURES TO PROMOTE AND REGULATE
FOREIGN DIRECT INVESTMENT IN DEVELOPING COUNTRIES

a)   By DAC Home Countries

Most OECD governments encourage direct investment flows to developing countries, seeking a positive contribution to the host country's economy, benefits for the home country (improved export opportunities, preferential access to natural resources, including energy) and positive international economic interdependence more generally. However, under increasing domestic pressure some home countries have adopted a more neutral policy concerning investment abroad.

---

2. See the CIME's recent report "International Investment and Multinational Enterprises: Recent International Direct Investment Trends", OECD, Paris 1981.
3. "Changing International Investment Strategies: the 'New Forms' of Investment in Developing Countries", OECD, Paris, 1982.

By the 1950s and 1960s the United States, the United Kingdom, Germany, Japan and France had established incentive schemes which offered a broad range of facilities to their investors in developing countries. Other DAC countries did not actively support the flow of foreign direct investment to developing countries until the early 1970s. They have not, on the other hand, restricted it. Since then, most of them have adopted incentive measures.

Investment incentives used and measures taken by Member countries to ensure equal treatment of capital invested abroad, and income derived from it, as compared to investment made, and investment income from "at home", can be grouped as follows:

i) Investment guarantee schemes covering "political" (as opposed to commercial) risks outside the investor's control. Only some 9 per cent of the total investment stock in developing countries held by enterprises from DAC countries is presently covered (with a widely varying ratio for individual home countries: France 4 per cent, Germany 10 per cent, Japan 53 per cent, the United Kingdom 2 per cent, the United States 7 per cent; see also Table 7. These low percentages reflect, at least in part, the fact that sizeable investments were made prior to the establishment of insurance schemes which only cover new investments, and also the fact that some of the large foreign investors prefer "self-insurance". Others seem to be discouraged from seeking guarantees on account of what they regard as excessive bureaucratic procedures or limitations inherent in the schemes.

ii) Fiscal measures: Preferential treatment for capital invested in developing countries through "tax deferral". "Tax credit systems", generally not restricted to investment in developing countries and in use by most OECD Members allow the investor to deduct foreign taxes paid on investment income from his national income tax on the basis of national legislation or bilateral treaties for the avoidance of double taxation. Other fiscal measures relevant for foreign direct investment are the tax exemption method, the international affiliation privilege and the fictitious tax credit(4)

4. For a detailed description see Eugen Jehle, "Tax Incentives of Industrialised Countries for Private Undertakings in Developing Countries", in Bulletin for International Fiscal Documentation, 1982, No. 3, Amsterdam, March 1982.

iii) Information and promotion activities, particularly the partial and reimbursable financing of
pre-investment and feasibility studies. These
programmes have been expanded in recent years,
notably in Germany, Japan and the United States.

iv) Official financial support for private enterprises investing in developing countries.
Examples are "Starting Aid Projects" (Austria),
"Second Rank Loans" (France), loans for the
establishment in developing countries for small
and medium-sized investors (Germany), lending
by six Japanese public financial institutions
(including Eximbank and OECF) to Japanese
entrepreneurs and United States "Cooley" loans.

v) Activities of Public Development Finance Corporations (the bilateral equivalent to the
IFC), at present established by ten DAC Members. These institutions have a dual function
as investment banks and development institutions, with a considerable leverage in mobilising other foreign and local capital.

A number of DAC countries have concluded bilateral
investment promotion and protection agreements with developing countries, and the network of such agreements is
still growing. They are designed to secure protection
against discriminatory action by the host country, with
respect to both local firms and to investors from other
countries. Foreign investment covered by the agreements
is not exempt from expropriation/nationalisation, but the
host country agrees to provide in such cases adequate,
prompt and transferable compensation. Most investment
protection agreements contain arbitration clauses for
cases of litigation, often by reference to the rules of
the International Centre for the Settlement of Investment
Disputes (ICSID) established under the aegis of the World
Bank. In case of investment agreements concluded between
an EEC-Member state and an associated developing country,
the agreement of LOME II stipulates that the host country
will extend the provisions of such agreements to investments from other EEC Member States.

b)   Official Measures by Developing Host Countries

Host country policies often present a mixture of
measures designed to attract as well as to restrict
foreign direct investment. Major concerns of developing
host countries with foreign(5) direct investment stem

_____

5. These concerns seem to apply exclusively to
investments from industrialised countries, whereas the
(Continued on next page.)

from the following considerations:

    a) products produced by the foreign investor cater
       mainly to the better-off consumers;
    b) the technology employed may not be suitable to
       the factor endowment of their host countries;
    c) profits may be excessive because the foreign in-
       vestor insists on protection by restrictions on
       competitive imports;
    d) foreign firms may engage in restrictive business
       practices and conceal profits through non-"arm's
       length" transfer prices; and
    e) large foreign firms often have privileged access
       to local capital giving them a competitive advan-
       tage over local firms.

    It cannot be stated too strongly that, to attract
foreign investment, the host country's overall economic
policies are of crucial importance and that special incentives play only a subsidiary role. Industrialising
developing countries with large and rapidly expanding
markets and with a highly productive labour force are in
a strong position when negotiating with foreign and international enterprises, and in imposing sectoral or
other limitations (e.g. ownership restrictions and performance requirements) on their activities in the host
country. There are, however, still many developing countries with limited market potential, small resource
endowments and without a strong and effective administration, which are not yet able to negotiate with multinational enterprises from a position of strength.

    Developing countries often try to attract foreign
investment by offering a wide range of incentives including tax concessions, official financial support and other
measures pertaining to exchange controls, labour and environmental standards. Because of growing competition
among developing countries for foreign investment, many
host governments now offer a similar range of costly in-
centives(6) which, therefore, tend to be self-defeating.
With better general economic policies and a better entry
system, the same amount of investment could be attracted
at a lower cost. Tax incentives appear to be a particularly inappropriate way of attracting foreign investment
in cases where the incentive consists of foregone tax

(Note 5 continued from previous page.)
emerging multinational enterprises from more advanced
developing countries e.g. India, South Korea, apparently
do not raise similar objections by developing host
countries.
    6. See: "Investment Laws of the World" compiled and
classified by the International Centre for Settlement of
Investment Disputes (ICSID), Oceana Publications, Inc.
Dobbs Ferry, New York.

revenue but where the home country of the investor, in assessing the latter's taxable world income, allows only the deduction of foreign taxes actually paid, thus eliminating the incentive character of the host countries' tax policy.

Many developing countries use performance-oriented policies designed to control the operations of foreign firms, for example by requiring them to use domestic inputs and labour or to engage local management partners, and by controlling their access to the local financial markets. Sometimes a minimum share of exports is also imposed on the production of foreign enterprises.

Performance requirements are often combined with outright restrictions for foreign investors, barring them from "sensitive" sectors (e.g. defence, public utilities). In some countries, foreign banks and insurance companies are also restricted in their activities, despite - and sometimes because of - the considerable expansion of branches and subsidiaries of international banks in developing countries during the last decade. Moreover, in a large number of developing countries, foreign industrial ownership is now limited to minority participation, with exceptions sometimes permitted if the country wants to attract particularly useful investments with a high technology content or large foreign exchange earnings. Other restrictions pertain to the repatriation of capital and profits and to price controls.

Some host countries apply investment incentives side by side with performance requirements and investment restrictions. The net effect is often discouraging for the potential foreign investor who seeks clear and transparent conditions.

4. TRENDS OF FOREIGN DIRECT INVESTMENT DURING THE 1970s

a) The Data Base

Any review and analysis of foreign direct investment trends encounters formidable statistical and definitional difficulties. In recent years, there was a significant change in the pattern of financing of foreign ventures through "direct" investment, with a shift from equity participation to a greater use of loans and supplier credits. Another shift occurred in that direct control by the parent company gave way to management participation, technical assistance and training arrangements, production-sharing and supply contracts, and other "new forms" of investment.

The term "foreign direct investment" currently in use, implying a substantive portion of equity participation and effective control of the management, does not cover these changes: thus, statistical series based only on equity definitions no longer fully reflect the economic realities of foreign investment flows. Apart from these conceptual problems, there are difficulties in comparing direct investment data from individual DAC countries. Each country defines "direct" investment differently, either by a minimum percentage of equity and other long-term capital in the foreign venture (ranging from about 10 to 50 per cent), or by applying the IMF definition(7). The changes mentioned above also affect the volume of the accumulated stock of foreign investments, for which at present only rough estimates of book value are available. These are mainly based on an OECD survey of a sample of enterprises in Member countries with subsequent additions of new flows and adjustments where possible(8).

A related statistical problem concerns the assessment of reinvested earnings for which estimates have to be made by the Secretariat where no information from DAC Members is available. For example, data on foreign direct investment flows to developing countries from the United States, which currently represent over half of the DAC total, suggest that roughly some 40 per cent of net foreign direct investments are reinvested earnings. (This share is significantly lower than for U.S. foreign direct investment in industrialised countries.)

b)   DAC Member Source Countries

Annual direct investment flows to developing countries grew at a fairly rapid pace thoughout the last decade to some $15 billion in 1981, with an "accidental"

---

7. The IMF Balance of Payments Manual (4th ed. 1977, paragraph 408) defines foreign direct investment as: "investment that is made to acquire a lasting interest in an enterprise operating in an economy other than that of the investor, the investor's purpose being to have an effective voice in the management of the enterprise". The Group of Financial Statisticians of the OECD Committee on Financial Markets reached agreement, in 1981, on an operational definition of foreign direct investment, using the 10 per cent cut-off point (applied in Canada, the United States and for the purpose of most double taxation agreements). Member countries are considering implementing the recommendations of the Group.
8. Stock of Private Direct Investment by DAC Countries in Developing Countries, End of 1969, OECD, Paris 1972 (out of print).

Table 1

NET DIRECT INVESTMENT FLOWS FROM DAC COUNTRIES TO DEVELOPING COUNTRIES, 1971-1981

$ million

DAC Country	1971	1972	1973	1974	1975	1976	1977	1978	1979	1980	1981
Australia	48	102	104	117	48	75	84	68	113	136	159
Austria	-	4	5	8	7	33	18	20	13	20	32
Belgium	29	58	48	50	69	236	70	138	254	198	123
Canada	76	176	125	193	293	253	360	558	-100	400	700
Denmark	25	10	16	26	30	30	-	77	66	79	66
Finland	1	1	x	x	3	1	2	6	15	26	17
France	170	231	287	239	274	245	265	413	681	900	1,137
Germany	358	601	787	701	816	765	846	1,025	818	1,579	1,352
Italy	214	280	246	100	150	213	162	71	455	316	132
Japan	222	204	1,301	705	223	1,084	724	1,318	691	906	2,426
Netherlands	130	321	89	242	229	245	486	444	167	135	354
New Zealand	-	-2	1	3	1	1	9	11	7	24	15
Norway	11	7	14	15	17	43	16	30	8	9	8
Sweden	40	42	22	49	82	125	126	115	127	90	86
Switzerland	66	73	81	128	208	226	211	174	416	353	340
United Kingdom(1)	233	391	699	695	653	838	1,179	820	1,029	1,047	1,217
United States	1,686	1,736	895	-2,172	7,241	3,119	4,866	5,619	7,986	3,367	6,475
Total DAC	3,309	4,235	4,720	1,100	10,344	7,534	9,424	10,907	12,746	9,585	14,639

1. Excluding investment in the petroleum sector.

break of the trend in 1973/1975 (due to abnormally high oil-disinvestment in 1973 and 1974, in particular by U.S. firms in the Middle East, and heavy reinvestment by the oil industry, in 1975, in other regions of the Third World). Figures for 1980 ($10 billion) indicate another "break" probably also due to several take-overs of oil assets in that year. From 1971 to 1981, the average annual growth rate of net foreign direct investment flows was 14 per cent (some 5 per cent in constant prices). Details of individual DAC Members' investment flows during the decade are set out in Table 1 and Table 2.

Throughout the past decade, the United States played a dominant role among DAC countries by providing about one-half of all foreign direct investment flows to developing countries. Germany, France, Japan and the United Kingdom were other important source countries. In particular Japan, France and Switzerland showed a higher than average growth of investment flows during the decade, whereas flows from the Netherlands, Italy and Australia stagnated and decreased in real terms.

Among the factors influencing investment decisions, geographical proximity, historical ties and trade relations play an important role. This is in addition to the fundamentals: the investors' profitability perception and the investment climate in the host country. The geographical distribution pattern of investment flows from major DAC countries is shown below:

DISTRIBUTION OF GEOGRAPHICALLY ALLOCATED DIRECT
INVESTMENT FLOWS (NET) FROM MAJOR SOURCE COUNTRIES,
1979-81(1)

Percentages

	Europe	Africa	Latin America	Asia	Total
France	33 (34)	23 (16)	39 (6)	5 (2)	100
Germany	21 (18)	5 (3)	59 (7)	15 (4)	100
Japan	1 (4)	9 (16)	29 (11)	61 (49)	100
U.K.(2)	10 (13)	30 (25)	36 (7)	24 (9)	100
U.S.	5 (31)	9 (40)	69 (69)	17 (36)	100
Total 5 countries	(100)	(100)	(100)	(100)	(100)

1. Figures in brackets denote the home countries' share in the total foreign direct investment of the continent from the five source countries, including official support for private investment by the Japanese Government.
2. Excluding investments in the oil industry.

The accumulated <u>stock</u> of foreign direct investment in developing countries which is controlled by firms from DAC countries represented a book-value of some $137 billion at the end of 1981. The distribution of the stock among source countries is set out in Table 3, and its comparison with the investment stock at the end of 1970 reveals the rapidly growing importance of Germany and Japan as sources of private investment while traditional large sources of direct investment, such as the United States, the United Kingdom, France and the Netherlands, saw their shares reduced correspondingly.

c)   Developing Host Countries

Whereas the statistical coverage of foreign direct investment flows to different geographic regions is fairly complete, there are serious data gaps with respect to the distribution to individual host countries and, hence, groups of such countries. Only about 80 per cent of the total flow in recent years can be allocated in this way. Moreover, a significant distortion of investment statistics stems from the fact that a considerable portion of foreign direct investment funds flows to affiliates in third countries, to offshore banking centres and "tax havens" to be reinvested subsequently, at least in part, in other host countries, developed and developing alike, without clear statistical evidence of their final distribution.

With these limitations in mind, it can be stated that the eleven newly-industrialising countries [NICs(9)] accounted for more than half of total DAC direct investment flows in recent years. Middle-Income Countries (MICs) were the second largest group of recipients, but their receipts are dominated by off-shore banking centres. Low-income countries (LICs) captured only a marginal portion of foreign direct investment. The 13 OPEC Members recorded a temporary drop in their direct investment receipts in 1979 due to the developments in Iran and disinvestments in Indonesia and Nigeria. For more details, see Table 4 and the following summary.

The People's Republic of China, which does not belong to any of the groupings mentioned above, receives growing amounts of direct investment ($200 million in 1979, and $550 million in 1980, over $2 billion in 1981). China is likely to attract more direct investment in the future since its Foreign Investment Law of 1979 and subsequent regulations confirmed the importance

---

9. Argentina, Brazil, Greece, Hong Kong, Korea Rep., Mexico, Portugal, Singapore, Spain, Taiwan, Yugoslavia. For other country groupings, see the DAC list of country groups in Table 10.

Table 2

NET DIRECT INVESTMENT FLOWS FROM DAC COUNTRIES TO
DEVELOPING COUNTRIES, 1970-1981,
INDIVIDUAL COUNTRIES' SHARES AND GROWTH RATES

Percentages

DAC Country	Share in Investment Flow		Average Annual Growth Rate
	1970-72	1979-81	1970/72-1979/81
Australia	2.3	1.1	5
Austria	x	0.2	25
Belgium	1.2	1.6	18
Canada	2.8	2.7	14
Denmark	0.4	0.6	19
Finland	x	0.2	76
France	5.7	7.3	18
Germany	11.4	10.1	13
Italy	5.5	2.4	4
Japan	6.1	10.9	22
Netherlands	5.6	1.8	0
New Zealand		0.1	n.a.
Norway	0.3	0.1	-4
Sweden	1.1	0.8	11
Switzerland	1.7	3.0	21
United Kingdom	8.6	8.9	15
United States	47.3	48.2	14
TOTAL DAC	100.0	100.0	14

China attaches to the participation of foreign capital in
the modernisation of the country's economy. China is
ready to accept, and will even require, a certain degree
of equity participation by its foreign partners in order
to ensure their identification with the joint ventures.

As shown below, developing countries' receipts of
direct foreign investment constitute an important share
of their total bilateral financial receipts from DAC Members and, of course, an even higher proportion of their
total non-concessional financial receipts. The drop in
the shares between the beginning and the end of the 1970s
is largely due to the upsurge of bank lending and export
credits in the financial flows to developing countries.

The distribution of the estimated stock of foreign
direct investment among developing host countries (see
Table 5) shows a clear preponderance of the NICs. At

SHARE OF DEVELOPING COUNTRY GROUPS IN ALLOCATED
DAC FOREIGN DIRECT INVESTMENT FLOWS (NET) 1977-81

percentages

	1977	1979	1981
LIC	8	5	4
MIC (of which off-shore centres)	19 (7)	31 (19)	27 (15)
NIC (11)	51	61	44
OPEC (13)	22	3	25
Total	<u>100</u>	<u>100</u>	<u>100</u>

NET FOREIGN DIRECT INVESTMENT RECEIPTS OF
DEVELOPING COUNTRIES AS A PERCENTAGE OF:

	Average 1970-72	Average 1979-81
Total Bilateral Financial Receipts	25%	18%
Non-concessional Bilateral Financial Receipts	55%	27%

the end of 1981, about 41 per cent of the total stock was
located in these eleven countries, in particular in the
three Latin American countries which accounted for 25 per
cent of the total (Brazil 13 per cent, Mexico 8 per cent,
Argentina 4 per cent). The four European NICs and the
four Far Eastern NICs shared the remaining 15 per cent
about equally. The dominant role of Brazil may be ex-
plained by the sheer size of the country as well as by
the investors' confidence in the country's growth and
resource potential, coupled with a liberal economic
policy which is expected to continue.

The group of MIC's represented over one third of the
total investment stock but nearly half of this amount was
accounted for by "tax havens" and off-shore banking
centres.

As one would expect, the LIC's hold only a small
portion of the total stock, with India alone representing
about one quarter of the group. The case of India is
interesting in that the nationalisation of foreign enterprises has apparently affected the overall stock of
foreign investment in the country less than is often

Table 3

DAC COUNTRIES' ESTIMATED STOCK OF DIRECT INVESTMENT IN DEVELOPING COUNTRIES, BY COUNTRY OF ORIGIN, END-1970 AND END-1981

DAC Country	$ million		Percentage of Total	
	1970	1981	1970	1981
Australia	305	1,359	1	1
Austria	15	175	x	x
Belgium	765	2,038	2	2
Canada	1,659	4,693	4	3
Denmark	45	470	x	x
Finland	1	73	x	x
France	3,832	8,674	9	7
Germany	1,942	11,590	4	9
Italy	1,245	3,584	3	3
Japan	1,218	11,022(1)	3	8
Netherlands	2,247	5,089	5	4
New Zealand	-	70	-	x
Norway	46	224	x	x
Sweden	305	1,209	1	1
Switzerland	875	3,151	2	2
United Kingdom	5,912	14,713	14	11
United States	22,300	63,118	52	48
Total DAC	42,712	131,252(1)	100.0	100

1. Excluding official support for private investment (some $6 billion).

claimed by the investment community. Moreover, India's present needs to increase energy production seem to have softened the hitherto rather restrictive policy in admitting new foreign investment. It can thus be expected that the financial and technological resources necessary for the development of the country's oil and coal potential will to a large extent come in the form of foreign direct investment.

The share of OPEC members in the total stock of direct investment is relatively small in relation to the wealth and growth potential of these countries. This is mainly due to the ongoing nationalisation of the foreign oil companies' assets since the first oil price shock, though accompanied in many cases by production sharing and other compensation agreements. As the Nigerian nationalisation measures in 1979 showed, this trend continues so that foreign direct oil investment in its traditional form might cease to exist in the future, with

Table 4

NET RECEIPTS OF GEOGRAPHICALLY ALLOCABLE DAC FOREIGN
DIRECT INVESTMENT
1978 to 1981
BY DEVELOPING COUNTRY GROUPS AND SELECTED RECIPIENTS

$ million

Group/Recipient		1978	1979	1980	1981
LICs		418	434	319	540
of which:	Egypt	22	38	27	120
	India	18	49	55	72
	Niger	20	9	- 5	-1
	Somalia	x	0	0	x
	Zaïre	98	144	111	67
MICs		1,666	2,796	2,768	3,680
of which:	Colombia	79	96	113	193
	Peru	66	326	98	231
	Philippines	144	330	125	110
	Thailand	38	38	217	218
Off-shore Banking Centres(1)		1,317	1,703	1,799	1,996
NICs		3,799	5,447	5,125	5,990
of which:	Argentina	310	667	880	638
	Brazil	1,738	1,533	788	1,256
	Hong Kong	252	342	363	964
	Korea	184	1	- 208	260
	Mexico	495	1,048	2,001	1,154
	Spain	527	1,233	486	415
OPEC		1,905	257	1,005	3,330
of which:	Gabon	9	20	25	27
	Indonesia	418	- 383	280	2,580
	Iran	909	164	81	24
	Nigeria	164	- 49	92	406
	S. Arabia	54	73	27	42
	Venezuela	184	131	99	296
Total allocated		7,788	8,934	9,217	13,540

1. Bahamas, Bermuda, Cayman Is., Liberia, Netherlands Antilles, Panama.

possible exceptions in smaller host countries. Current efforts to develop downstream industries in oil-producing countries follow a similar, though less pronounced, pattern since they are carried out mainly by national oil companies with minority foreign participation. On the other hand, service industries, in particular banking and insurance, are being built up rapidly in the Middle East which may leave room for foreign direct participation, though on a more modest scale.

d)   Distribution by Sector of Activity

Incomplete data prevent a detailed analysis of the distribution of foreign direct investment by sectors of developing countries' economies. Only five DAC Members, though accounting for the lion's share of total DAC investment flows and stock in developing countries, report sectoral destinations (see Table 6). However, these data are not fully comparable between reporting countries because of different coverage and other reasons. It is therefore only possible to review some large sectors: agriculture, petroleum, mining, manufacturing and "other industries".

For the five major source countries, manufacturing accounts for the largest share of both flows and stocks, with a bigger share in new flows than in the present stock. The same rising trend is discernible for direct foreign investment in "other industries", mainly service activities, including trade, finance and insurance. In contrast, the other sectors (agriculture, petroleum and gas, mineral mining, including coal) show a decreasing trend.

Concerning the sectoral distribution of investments from individual Member countries, one can point to the high shares of German and U.S. investment in manufacturing and to high shares of petroleum investment from Japan and France. Germany is also increasing its petroleum investment at the expense of investment in other mining sectors, in particular coal. Japanese investors, on the other hand, are providing a considerable and steady flow to the "other mining" sector.

As far as foreign investment in non-fuel minerals is concerned, there has been a worldwide slowdown during the 1970s which has given rise to concern about the adequacy of future (long-term) supply. This applies in particular to exploration activities in developing countries which stagnated or declined due to the persistent economic stagnation in OECD countries and for other reasons.

Finance is of crucial importance if mining investment is to be stepped up. It is doubtful in the absence of remunerative prices and/or long-term demand

Table 5

ESTIMATED STOCK(1) OF DAC DIRECT INVESTMENT IN
DEVELOPING COUNTRIES AT END-1981 BY COUNTRY GROUPS AND
SELECTED HOST COUNTRIES

(with stock - book value - exceeding $1 billion)

Group/Country		$ Billion	Percentage Share
LICs		10.2	7
of which:	India	2.7	
	Zaïre	1.6	
MICs		49.1	36
of which:	Bermuda*	5.5	
	Panama*	4.9	
	Bahamas*	3.8	
	Neth. Antilles*	3.7	
	Malaysia	3.5	
	Peru	3.0	
	Philippines	2.5	
	Columbia	2.0	
	Chile	2.0	
	Liberia*	1.7	
	Trinidad &		
	Tobago	1.3	
	Israel	1.2	
NICs		55.6	41
of which:	Brazil	17.2	
	Mexico	10.3	
	Spain	6.9	
	Argentina	5.6	
	Singapore	3.9	
	Hong Kong	3.8	
	Taiwan	2.3	
	Korea (South)	1.6	
	Greece	1.0	
OPEC		22.3	16
of which:	Indonesia	8.6	
	Venezuela	4.3	
	Nigeria	1.2	
	Libya	1.5	
Europe		11.5	9
Africa		15.5	11
Latin America		71.8	52
Asia		38.4	28
TOTAL		137.2	100

*) Offshore Banking Centre.
1. Including unallocated amounts and Japanese official
support for private investment.

Table 6

DAC FOREIGN DIRECT INVESTMENT IN DEVELOPING COUNTRIES, DISTRIBUTION BY
MAJOR SECTORS OF ACTIVITY AND SELECTED SOURCE COUNTRIES, RECENT FLOWS AND
ACCUMULATED STOCKS (VARIOUS YEARS)

Percentages

DAC Country	Agriculture		Petroleum (incl. gas)		Other Mining (incl. coal)		Manufacturing		Other	
	flow	stock	flow	stock	flow	stock	flow	stock	flow	stock
France	1	n.a.	34	n.a.	2	n.a.	26	n.a.	37	n.a.
Germany	1	1	9	6	- 3	1	53	62	40	30
Japan	2	3	35	35	6	6	38	37	19	19
U.K. (excl. petroleum)	n.a.	13	-	-	n.a.	4	n.a.	46	n.a.	37
U.S.	1	n.a.	- 38	10	2	8	60	39	75	43
Total (above)	1	2	8	14	1	6	47	42	43	36

commitments whether the huge funds required to create adequate future supply capacities (a large mining/ smelting complex costs about $1 billion) will come forward in time. Moreover, political risks have gained particular importance among criteria for mining investment in developing countries.

5. FUTURE OUTLOOK

To meet their needs in the 1980s, developing countries will have to continue to rely on substantial commercial financial flows, of which direct investment will play an increasingly important role. The growth trend of new foreign direct investment in recent years is encouraging and more favourable than the trends for some other types of external commercial finance. However, the long-term character of direct investment and its project orientation does not make it a suitable instrument for balance of payments financing. This holds true in particular if one takes into account the long lead times involved and the fact that around one third of new direct investment consists of retained profits, which do not represent a new external resource flow.

From the investors' side, there will probably be a continuing desire to expand investment abroad in order to benefit from comparative advantages. But investors will be increasingly selective regarding the location of their foreign ventures, comparing the situation of developing and developed countries carefully. Investors often require higher returns to compensate for the perceived higher risks of their investments in developing countries.

If the upward trend of foreign direct investment in developing countries is to remain a long-term feature of international economic relations, a convergence of attitudes in developing and developed countries concerning multinational enterprises would be an important prerequisite. International discussions and bilateral negotiations between home and host countries may help to achieve this objective. Barring major unexpected disturbances, average annual growth rates of DAC foreign investment in developing countries may be as high as in the past decade, notwithstanding considerable annual fluctuations.

Part II

SCHEMES OF INDIVIDUAL COUNTRIES AND INSTITUTIONS

A. SUMMARY

The governments of most DAC Member countries have developed policies for the stimulation of foreign direct investment in developing countries alongside the evolution of their programmes of official aid, given the complementarity of both resource flows in the development process. While official aid has gone predominantly to support the public sector investment, private investors have provided a sizeable external contribution to the directly productive sectors.

The authorisation of outward direct investment for exchange control (or other) purposes is to be granted under conditions set forth in the OECD Code of Liberalisation of Capital Movements of 1961(1) to which all DAC countries, except Canada, adhere. The Code stipulates that direct investment abroad by residents shall be free in principle. Some Member countries have lodged reservations on this item which will be withdrawn as Members are able to accept the liberalisation obligations under the Code. The Code also contains clauses of derogation which members can invoke if their economic and financial situation justifies such a course.

Most OECD countries retain partial or complete administrative systems for the control of capital outflows, although in many cases requests for bona fide direct investment are granted automatically or almost so. In general, direct investments in developing countries are

---

1. Code of Liberalisation of Capital Movements, OECD, Paris, updated edition March 1982. The OECD Committee on Capital Movements and Invisible Transactions has the general task of considering all questions concerning the interpretation or implementation of the provisions of the Code.

subject to only very limited restrictions. Moreover, some of the more important restrictions have resulted not so much in preventing investment projects from going ahead, but rather in forcing investors to use sources of international borrowing for their financing.

The existing incentive programmes, which vary to a large extent from one DAC country to another, can be grouped into the following categories:

a) investment guarantee schemes covering "political" or "non-commercial risks" - i.e. risks which are outside the investor's control;
b) fiscal treatment of investment income from developing countries;
c) information and promotion activities, particularly the financing of pre-investment and feasibility studies;
d) co-operation between government aid agencies and private foreign investors;
e) government-sponsored investment corporations.

It must be stressed that the possibilities for action on the part of the capital exporting countries to stimulate the flow of private capital to developing countries are rather limited. However elaborate the incentive measures introduced by DAC countries, the major responsibility for the improvement of the investment climate remains with the host countries. In the past, therefore, many developing countries have introduced general or selective measures for the attraction, protection and promotion of foreign investment, and have frequently refined them(2).

Private investors have indicated that they find certain types of incentives provided by capital-exporting countries particularly useful. There is evidence that investors take advantage of fiscal incentives, of guarantee programmes, of public-financed feasibility studies or partnership with public investment corporations. However, it is not possible to determine the quantitative impact of the measures on the volume of foreign direct investment in developing countries.

Increasing use of the various incentive programmes in recent years has resulted from their technical improvement, in turn made possible through experience in their operation. The governments of DAC Member countries exchange their experience in these fields on a continuing basis at the OECD. Their mutual co-operation has been

---

2. See: "Investment Laws of the World", compiled and classified by the International Centre for Settlement of Investment Disputes (ICSID), Oceana Publications, Inc./Dobbs Ferry, New York.

particularly helpful in the case of countries establishing new programmes.

A general summary of the various incentive programmes is provided below.

a)   Investment Guarantee Schemes(3)

All DAC Member countries have established investment
guarantee systems of general application covering non-
commercial risks. The schemes are sometimes restricted
to certain categories of investment, mostly related to
export operations. To date, experience has shown favourable reactions from investors, in particular for the
coverage of small and medium-sized investments. It
should be noted that investment guarantees are not always
specifically limited to investments in developing countries. All schemes have a common feature in that guarantees are available only for new investments, i.e. for new
projects or for expansion programmes (for amounts of investment under guarantee see Table 7, a list of guarantee
agencies is given in Table 8).

Type of risks insured

Under most programmes, the so-called non-commercial
or political risks covered by the schemes are grouped
into three categories:

- Expropriation risks: these include expropriation
  or nationalisation and confiscation without adequate compensation. In a number of schemes, the
  expropriatory action must have continued for at
  least one year before it is considered. While all
  schemes cover straight expropriation, the situation varies as regards cases of "creeping expropriation", where the local enterprise is not taken
  over but its operation is impeded by government
  action to a point where it can no longer operate
  effectively.
- War risks, including revolution, rebellion and
  civil war. In order to retain an element of risk
  equivalent to that in developed countries, destruction resulting from a general war is not in
  principle covered.

3. In a strict sense, the word "guarantee" refers to
full coverage of 100 per cent of the value of the investment made, as opposed to "insurance" which may cover only
a certain percentage of the investment. Although most
national schemes provide only limited coverage, the term
most currently used by governments and institutions is
"guarantee" and this generic term is used throughout this
survey.

- Transfer risks, essentially exchange control action taken after the conclusion of the guarantee
contract and preventing or delaying the repatriation of profits and capital. Under all schemes,
however, this category excludes the risk of de-
valuation of the local currency. Also, in most
programmes, local government action (other than
exchange controls), which impedes actual repatriation, falls under expropriation risks.

Type of investment guaranteed

Each scheme can provide coverage for different categories of capital participation in projects such as:
equity, inter-company lending, licences, royalties, etc.

Eligibility criteria

It is difficult to summarize the qualitative criteria which the various schemes demand of applications
for guarantees. Most guarantee programmes specifically
require that the investment projects further the economic
development of the host country or that the project under
consideration forms part of its development programme.
While the assessment of the developmental impact of investments may differ from one DAC country to another,
guarantee schemes generally require that the projects be
approved by the host government, at least in cases where
intergovernmental agreements or the regulations of the
developing countries require such an approval.

At the same time, many capital exporting countries
require that the projects provide economic advantages to
their own economies. In particular, certain countries
specifically cite the promotion of exports as an eligibility criterion.

In general, investment insurance portfolios are not
concentrated on large companies. In fact, foreign investments of many large multinational companies often are
not guaranteed at all against political risks.

Fees charged

Under some schemes, the three categories of risks
can be covered separately, while other schemes charge a
unique fee for the three risks combined (of around
0.5 per cent of principal). Fees normally are standard
fees although a number of schemes make provision for
lower or higher charges for particular situations or particular risks. Some countries offer premium rates for
investors in joint ventures with local partners.

Extent of guarantee coverage

Provision is generally made for writing down over time the value of the investment guaranteed. Some countries look to the financial statements as in periodically audited accounts, while others adopt fixed schedules for writing down their value. Of the value thus established, the investor under most schemes bears a fraction of the risk himself in case of a loss; and indemnities paid usually represent around 90 per cent of the loss.

The coverage of earnings can be defined either under a global ceiling (e.g. a percentage of the original investment) or under an annual limit (e.g. 8 per cent per annum for up to three years).

The maximum duration of coverage is usually between 15 to 20 years.

Prerequisite of investment protection agreements

Most DAC countries have concluded investment protection agreements with developing countries. Investment guarantees in these cases are provided, as a rule, only for investments in countries having signed such agreements. One of the main purposes of these agreements is to secure protection against discriminatory legal and administrative action, both as compared to the local business community and also as compared to investors from other countries. The agreements do not provide full and automatic protection against nationalisation. But the host country undertakes at least to provide fair compensation without undue delay. Agreements can be either detailed agreements of substance dealing with a number of issues such as guarantees, financial transfers, entry permission for foreign personnel, etc. or agreements limited to more procedural matters in the event that investments should be endangered.

Since these agreements appear to have provided effective protection for investments, as well as encouragement to foreign investors, new agreements continue to be negotiated and signed.

Guarantees for multinational projects

Large and medium-sized projects are increasingly being undertaken jointly by investors of more than one DAC country. With the present patchwork of national guarantee schemes, some investment partners can obtain investment guarantees but others cannot. Not only is there the problem of industrialised countries which have no scheme, but the definition of the "nationality" of the investing corporations used by the schemes is sometimes

Table 7

DIRECT INVESTMENT FROM DAC COUNTRIES IN DEVELOPING
COUNTRIES UNDER GUARANTEE AS OF 31st DECEMBER, 1981

DAC Member Country	Amount of investment covered(1) $ million	As share of total estimated stock of investment in LDCs per cent
Australia(*)	103	8
Austria	126	87
Belgium	34	2
Canada	105	3
Denmark	27	6
Finland	-	-
France	378	4
Germany	1,102	10
Italy	2	x
Japan	5,851	53
Netherlands	49	1
New Zealand	4	7
Norway	9	4
Sweden	n.a.	n.a.
Switzerland(**)	40	(1)
United Kingdom	250	2
United States(***)	4,098	(7)
Total DAC	(12,200)	(9)

1. Source: International Union of Credit and Investment
   Insurers (Berne Union)

(*) June 1982.
(**) End 1979.
(***) End 1980.

lacking in compatibility. The Finance Ministers of the EEC Member countries agreed therefore on a directive to permit transnational co-insurance in the EEC, which came into force in 1980.

b)   Fiscal measures

Problems regarding the desirability and character of fiscal incentives in capital-exporting countries for private investment in developing countries were the subject of comprehensive reviews by the OECD Committee on Fiscal Affairs in 1977 and the United Nations Group of Experts on Tax Treaties between Developed and Developing countries. For this reason the information provided in this survey on fiscal provisions and their effectiveness is limited(4).

There are several DAC countries which, upon acknowledging that taxes are paid abroad, exempt foreign income or offer a credit against foreign tax levied on world income. In other countries, foreign taxes may only be deducted as expenses, thereby leaving foreign investment at a disadvantage (tax exemptions granted by a developing country may be nullified with the result of higher tax liabilities in the capital-exporting country). It must also be pointed out that special tax incentives for domestic investment tend to work as a disincentive to foreign investment. Thus, foreign investment in developing countries may be less attractive than investment at home or in other industrialised countries in the absence of adequate tax treaties. Until recent years, developing countries themselves appear to have been reluctant to conclude treaties because the present pattern of tax conventions relies mainly on taxation in the country of residence and tends to favour capital-exporting countries. The United Nations Expert Group has formulated guidelines and techniques designed to be acceptable to both developing and developed countries for use in tax treaties.

At present, conventions signed between developed

----

4. Detailed information is provided in a number of specialised studies, in particular Fiscal Incentives for Private Investment in Developing Countries 1965, by the OECD Fiscal Committee; the Model Double Taxation Convention on Income and Capital 1977, by the OECD Committee on Fiscal Affairs; and the United Nations Model Double Taxation Convention between Developed and Developing Countries, New York, 1980. See also: United Nations Model Convention for Tax Treaties between Developed and Developing Countries, A description and analysis, by S. Surrey, Amsterdam 1980 (published by the International Bureau of Fiscal Documentation).

and developing countries follow the structure and a number of substantive provisions of the OECD Model Double Taxation Convention. However, as was envisaged by the OECD Committee on Fiscal Affairs, the majority of such conventions allocate greater taxing rights to the developing country for dividends, interest, royalties and technical services than the OECD Model. The definition of what constitutes a permanent establishment is also generally wider than in the OECD Model. In addition, a number of these conventions contain tax sparing or other special provisions.

c)   Investment Information and Promotion Activities

Investment opportunities in developing countries may remain unused if potential investors are inadequately informed. More active information programmes by capital-exporting and, perhaps even more, by capital-importing countries are therefore necessary to make businessmen familiar with economic conditions and opportunities in developing countries.

The basic services in this field offered by the governments of industrialised countries are provided by the traditional economic and commercial information centres to be found in the national administrations and in specialised agencies at home and diplomatic missions abroad. External trade services being mainly concerned with the promotion of exports, most DAC countries have now developed information systems for the dissemination of investment possibilities to national investors. Moreover, many DAC governments provide funds for the financing of pre-investment surveys and feasibility studies. Governments only finance a part - usually 50 per cent - of the cost of the survey, and the potential investor may have to reimburse its share of the cost, if the project materialises.

d)   Co-operation between Government Aid Agencies and Private Investors

Most DAC governments co-operate with private firms active in developing countries by offering both financial aid and technical assistance. Special programmes or funds for government loans to firms from DAC countries wishing to invest in developing countries have been set up e.g. in Austria, France, Germany, Japan and the United States. In addition, loans are sometimes extended to private firms operating in developing countries out of the ordinary aid programmes. Moreover, most countries have official export credit programmes helping to finance equipment exports(5). In some cases such export credits have been decisive factors in the financing of a private foreign investment.

e)   Government-sponsored Investment Corporations

Ten OECD countries, all Members of the DAC, and the World Bank have established special public development finance corporations (see list in Table 8)(6). These institutions invest directly in projects, usually in partnership with local and foreign investors. Most of them can invest in both loans and equity and do not ask for guarantees from the local government nor even, normally, for collateral for their loans. However, all institutions require host government approval of the projects they finance.

These corporations have been able to associate their limited public resources with a much larger volume of private funds. They perform a multiple role in promoting projects which are both commercially viable and have a developmental priority. First, they provide capital and related financial services, as well as technical assistance. But perhaps more important is their catalytic role. Far more involved than ordinary banking institutions in the evaluation of projects and overall financial arrangements, the corporations have frequently been responsible for bringing in other national and international investment partners. They are specifically intended to mobilise the flow of private capital from their own countries, but can also associate with investors from other developed countries. The International Finance Corporation, (IFC), the only multilateral institution of this kind, finances projects jointly with investors from any Member country of the World Bank.

Investors from the developed world trust and appreciate these public investment corporations because of their rigorous standards of financial appraisal and because they also bring a certain degree of security to investments in view of their official status. Local governments see in the participation of such an institution an assurance of "good developmental behaviour" on

---

5. For more detail see: "The Export Credit Financing Systems in OECD Member Countries", OECD, Paris 1982.
6. In addition, there are private investment companies, sponsored by the business community, which are organised either on a national or on a multinational basis: examples of the first category are the Commonwealth Development Finance Company in the United Kingdom and COFIMER in France. An example of a successful private multinational institution is the Private Investment Company for Asia S.A. (PICA) in Japan.

the part of the foreign enterprise. Their participation
also improves the standing of the enterprise with the
banking community and the relationships between local and
foreign investors.

The public corporations need to strike a careful
balance between their dual objectives as both investment
banks and development institutions. On the one hand,
they are expected to operate on commercial lines and pay
their own way, making profitable investments and thus
offering an attractive basis for the association of outside resources. On the other hand, they are instruments
of official development policy and are therefore concerned with developmental considerations. This implies
that they normally restrict their intervention to priority sectors and projects, and abstain from a number of
profitable projects which are not of clear developmental
priority or which do not require long-term financial assistance (trade, export, import, real estate, etc.). To
date, their activity has been concentrated in manufacturing, energy, public utilities, agriculture, agro-business
(particularly fertilizers), housing and tourism. While
the ventures they assist are expected to operate commercially and to maximise profits, the institutions themselves are not expected to maximise their own profits and
thus can provide financial services, technical and - for
some top priority projects - financial assistance on
relatively soft terms. The costs of these services are
not generally imputed to the projects financed.

Table 8

OFFICIAL INSTITUTIONS IN DAC MEMBER COUNTRIES
EXTENDING INVESTMENT FINANCE AND GUARANTEES(1)

OECD Member country	Public Development Finance Corporation	Guarantee Agency
Australia	-	EFIC
Austria	-	OKB
Belgium	SBI	OND
Canada	-	EDC
Denmark	IFU	DANIDA IFU
Finland	FINNFUND	VTL
France	CCCE BFCE FAC	COFACE BFCE
Germany	DEG	TREUARBEIT
Italy	-	SACE
Japan	EXIM OECF JICA JODC	EXIM EID/MITI
Netherlands	FMO	NCM
New Zealand	-	EXGO
Norway	-	GIEK
Sweden	SWEDFUND	EKN
Switzerland	-	GERG
United Kingdom	CDC	ECGD
United States	OPIC	OPIC

1. For detailed description of the institutions,
see the corresponding country sections.

B. INDIVIDUAL SCHEMES

1. AUSTRALIA

Exchange Control

Exchange control approvals for direct investment abroad are conditional on any return of capital being remitted to Australia together with all net earnings although necessary retentions for financing growth in working capital and for firmly planned future expansion are permitted. Investments involving a significant degree of Australian managerial participation and the export of managerial or technical skills, and investments which promote Australian exports or which protect existing Australian investment abroad, are normally permitted.

Bilateral Investment Protection Agreements

So far, Australia has not signed any specific agreements with developing countries for the protection of foreign direct investment.

Investment Guarantee Scheme

The Overseas Investment Insurance Scheme which was established in 1966 is administered on the Government's behalf by the Export Finance and Insurance Corporation (EFIC)(1). It provides investment insurance against the three main categories of non-commercial risk, separately or combined. In 1974, in conformity with its announced policy of encouraging Australian direct investment abroad (made with local participation, with the approval of the host country and in Australia's national interest), the government liberalised the criteria applying to investment eligible for insurance. In 1976 amendments were

---

1.EFIC, Export House, 22 Pitt Street, Sydney, N.S.W., Telephone 231 2655, Telex AA21224.

made to the legislation, providing for the expedited processing of the more routine applications for coverage by
permitting EFIC to insure these on its own account without reference to the Government for individual approval.

The investments eligible for coverage may consist of
equity participation or loans, and the form of transfer
may be cash, machinery, equipment, and technical or managerial services. The insurance may cover up to 200 per
cent of the value of the original investment (the "maximum amount" of insurance) to allow for insurance of accumulated earnings. The difference between the "maximum
amount" and the "current amount" (which is the coverage
provided on the basis of the current value of the investment over time), known as the "stand-by amount", provides
a reserve which the investor may use to insure the in-
creases in his participation in the foreign enterprise.
Remitted earnings eligible for insurance are not subject
to any limitation other than the maximum set for the
overall amount and duration of the insurance, but the
investor must attempt to transfer investment earnings
within nine months of receipt. The liability in the
event of loss will normally be not more than 90 per cent
of the insured amount, the investor bearing the remaining
10 per cent. The coverage is normally extended for a
minimum of 5 years and a maximum of 15 years. The premium for the three risks combined is 1.0 per cent annually plus 0.5 per cent of the "stand-by" amount. Each of
the three risks can be insured separately at a premium of
0.4 per cent with respect to expropriation risk and
0.3 per cent for each of the war and transfer risks on
the "current amount" and at half these rates on the
"stand-by". As the Australian Government considers it
desirable to foster local participation in the foreign
enterprise, a lower premium applies to joint ventures
with local investors, if the latter in principle own at
least 25 per cent of the enterprise (0.8 per cent on current amount for the combined risks and 0.4 per cent on
the stand-by amount).

The maximum contingent liability of EFIC on its own
and the Government's behalf is A$200 million. This
amount has not varied since it has been laid down by
legislation in 1974.

The total value of outstanding political insurance
policies at the end of June 1982 was $A118 million
(US$103) of which 90 per cent was in countries of South
East Asia (Members of ASEAN).

Fiscal Measures

Australian fiscal law makes no distinction between
income from industrialised and developing countries.
Dividends on foreign investment paid to Australian

40

companies are generally relieved from Australian tax by means of a rebate, whether or not tax is due in the country of origin. Dividends on foreign investment (including those received from Papua New Guinea) paid to Australian individuals and income other than wages and salaries earned in Papua New Guinea, as well as interest and royalty payments on which the foreign tax is limited under a double taxation agreement, are subject to Australian tax. But relief from double taxation is provided by means of a credit against Australian tax. Other foreign income of Australian residents which is not exempt from tax in the country of origin is at present exempt from taxation in Australia.

Double taxation agreements (with Singapore, Malaysia and the Philippines) provide for a tax sparing credit to be allowed to a resident of Australia against Australian tax with respect to interest and royalties (royalties only with the Philippines agreement) from the signatory countries for taxes foregone by those countries under their economic incentives legislation.

Other Official Support

In 1981 the Australian Development Assistance Bureau (ADAB) introduced a joint venture scheme into its South Pacific Aid Program. The aim of the scheme is to facilitate the creation of employment and generation of income in South Pacific countries through the establishment or expansion of businesses. It does this by using aid funds to assist South Pacific countries purchase equity in joint business ventures with Australian businesses. These funds are channelled through individual Island Governments in support of specific joint venture proposals. Although funds are not used to support the Australian partner in joint ventures, the effect of the scheme is to encourage investment by Australian partners.

The Department of Trade and Resources with its Trade Commissioner service provides potential investors with detailed information of regulations, incentives and opportunities available in other countries.

2. AUSTRIA

Exchange Control

The transfer of capital for direct investment abroad is subject to the approval of the Austrian National Bank. The authorisation will be granted provided the investment will result in the establishment and maintainance of commercial relations with Austria.

Investment Protection Agreements

So far, Austria has not signed any specific agreements for the protection of foreign direct investment with developing countries.

Investment Guarantee Scheme

The Austrian investment guarantee scheme which is administered by the Oesterreichische Kontrollbank (OKB)(1), applies to both industrialised and developing countries. It normally covers 90 to 100 per cent of the initial new investment in the form of equity participation, loans and licences. The investor may obtain an extension of the guarantee to include reinvested earnings. The premium for the coverage of the three main political risks combined is 0.5 per cent annually The maximum duration of the cover is 20 years. The total value of investment in developing countries covered at the end of 1981 was $126 million.

Fiscal Measures

Austria has signed a number of agreements on the avoidance of double taxation which are based on the principle of taxation at the source (i.e. profits earned and taxed in other countries are not taxable in Austria). Agreements of this kind are in force with Brazil, Egypt, Greece, India, Indonesia, Israel, Mexico, Pakistan,

---

1. OKB, Am Hof 4, P.O. Box 70, A-1011 Vienna, Telephone: 66270; Telex: 13-27 85; Cable: Kontrollbank Wien.

Portugal, Spain, Turkey. In order to minimise double taxation of income earned in countries other than those mentioned above, an investor mayapply to the financial authorities. A further facility is provided by the income-tax law, which stipulates that investments made for the sale, installation or servicing of products made in Austria may be valued, for tax purposes, at 90 per cent of their costs. However, to benefit from this regulation, the participation of the Austrian investor has to exceed 25 per cent of the total capital of the foreign company.

Other Official Support

In order to promote the activities of Austrian enterprises in developing countries, the OKB initiated in 1964 a credit programme called "Start-up assistance" (Starthilfe Kreditaktion) with ERP (European Recovery Programme) funds and financial assistance by the Federal Economic Chamber. The credits are administered by a Committee composed of representatives from the Federal Chancellery (Development Assistance Office), the Ministries of Finance, Trade and Foreign Affairs, as well as from the Federal Economic Chamber. The Committee evaluates each investment project with particular regard to its effect on the economy of the host country. Preferential treatment is given to joint ventures with local investors. The allocated amount which may be borrowed for up to ten years, with a grace period of up to five years, should be covered by an investment guarantee. State subsidies enable the Kontrollbank to extend loans on relatively favourable terms at an interest rate of 5 to 6.5 per cent p.a. In 1974, the start-up credit scheme was reorganised and extended by the use of funds from the OKB's export financing scheme. From the end of 1977 onwards, start-up credits are available in the form of refinancing credits to credit institutes. New credits extended in 1981 amounted to AS42.3 million ($2.7 million).

The OKB also offers another form of financing of investment abroad which is not restricted to developing countries. Most of the conditions of these credits are similar to those of the "start-up" credits, but with higher interest rates. This instrument was added to the former so as to enable the Kontrollbank to provide loans for projects requiring large amounts of finance. In fact, the two lending programmes may be combined to finance particularly large enterprises.

Finally, the Austrian development assistance programme provides funds for feasibility and pre-investment studies.

3. BELGIUM

Exchange control

No authorisation is necessary in order to carry out a direct investment abroad but the investor must submit a written declaration indicating the purpose of the operation to a bank approved by the Belgium-Luxembourg Exchange Institute. Based upon this declaration, the bank automatically makes the transfer over the free exchange market. For investments considered to create or maintain lasting economic relations between the investor and the enterprise abroad, transfers via the official exchange market may be approved.

Bilateral investment protection agreements

Belgium has signed investment protection agreements with Cameroon, Egypt, Indonesia, Malaysia, Morocco, Romania, Singapore, South Korea, Tunisia and Zaire.

Investment guarantee scheme

The scheme guaranteeing Belgian direct investment abroad against political risk was established in 1971. Although applicable throughout the world, the scheme is of particular importance for investment in developing countries. The scheme is administered by the National Delcredere Office (Office National du Ducroire)(1), which also guarantees private export credits. The Board of Directors of the OND includes representatives of various Ministries (Economic Affairs, Finance, Foreign Trade) and of the General Administration for Development Co-operation. For an investment to be eligible for a guarantee, the OND applies two general criteria: (1) the project must make a contribution to the economic and social development of the recipient country and (2) it must promote Belgium's foreign economic relations. In addition, the investment must have the approval of the host country and must either be protected by the laws of that country, or by a bilateral agreement between Belgium and the other country.

---

1. OND, Square de Meeûs 40, 1040 Brussels.

The guarantee covers the three main categories of political risk and occasionally also "catastrophe risk" of unforseeable natural disasters. The coverage applies both to the initial amount of new investment and to rein-vested earnings, with a maximum of 50 per cent of the initial amount of investment. It may also cover distri-buted profits up to 10 per cent per annum of the capital sum insured. The guarantee covers 90 per cent of the amount insured, to be reduced to 80, 70 and 60 per cent respectively during the last three years of insurance.

The maximum duration of the guarantee is 15 years from the date of completion of the investment or 20 years from the date of issue of the policy. The premium for all risks combined is 0.75 per cent p.a. of the current amount or 0.8 per cent if earnings are included. At the end of 1981, the OND had outstanding investment insurance policies for a total of $34 million.

Fiscal Measures

In the absence of double taxation agreements, Belgian taxes on foreign earnings, which have already been taxed abroad, are reduced to one-quarter or one-half of the normal amount depending on wether the recipient is a company or an individual. Where double taxation agree-ments exist, such income is taxed in the foreign country only. Belgium has signed double taxation agreements with India, Indonesia, Israel, Malaysia, Morocoo, Singapore, Tunisia, Philippines, Republic of Korea, Pakistan, Thailand, Turkey, Zaire.

In practice Belgium already unilaterally exempts from all tax the dividends from permanent holdings, of whatever extent, in foreign companies (e.g. dividends from foreign subsidiaries). Under ordinary law, Belgium reduces the tax on other foreign investment income by 15 per cent of the net income after foreign tax. In the tax conventions with developing countries Belgium further applies the principle of the "tax sparing credit" or notional credit thus offsetting against its own tax, within certain limits, the taxes temporarily forgone by the developing countries as a stimulus to investment.

The Fund for Development Co-operation, FCD

Belgium has recently established, by law of 10th August, 1981, a "Fonds de la Coopération au Dévelop-pement" (FCD) which will become operational in early 1983. The Fund, to be administered by the General Ad-ministration for Development Co-operation, constitutes a new tool for financing productive investment in develop-ing countries through participation in national or regional development banks or in public or semi-public enterprises, mainly in the manufacturing sector(2). The financial resources of the Fund will come from the Belgian aid budget and are estimated to amount, in 1983, to BF9 billion ($200 million).

In creating the FCD Belgium has complemented its institutions in the area of promoting Belgian investment abroad. The "Société Belge pour l'Investissement International" (SBI, see below) was, in fact, created with the purpose of financing foreign investment both in developing and developed countries in order to support Belgian interests abroad, whereas the FCD is supposed to promote economic and social development in the Third World. Thus, projects to be financed by the Fund have to satisfy developmental considerations but have also to be economically viable. The host countries of the Fund's investments are expected to provide adequate protection of foreign investment including the possibility for repatriation of capital and earnings.

Target countries for the activities of the FCD are mainly those with whom Belgium has concluded co-operation agreements. At least 25 per cent of the Fund's resources will be devoted to projects in low-income countries. Financial support by the Fund can take the form of loans, interest subsidies or equity participation. Loans, or credit lines, will be provided at terms varying according to the nature of the projects and the stage of development of the recipient countries, but with a grant element of at least 25 per cent. Subsidies of up to 3 per cent will be granted on interest due for loans taken up for productive investment purposes; the Fund can also provide guarantees for loans which are eligible for an interest subsidy. Equity participation in enterprises can be constituted also by transforming financial outlays, by the FCD, for feasibility studies into an equity share for the Fund. Should the project not be executed the Fund and its partners will share the cost of the study.

Financial co-operation between the FCD and semi-public enterprises in developing countries will be governed by the following rules:

- the public sector must hold a majority participation in the enterprise ("public sector", for this purpose, being a public or semi-public enterprise, an enterprise whose liabilities are guaranteed by the state, or a national or regional development bank);

---

2. Under provisional arrangements, Belgium has already taken participations in the development banks of Rwanda, Burundi and of the States of the Great Lakes.

- the contribution by the Fund must at least amount to 10 per cent, but cannot exceed 30 per cent of the capital;
- private Belgian investment must at least equal the Fund's contribution (exception: investment in the least developed countries);
- Belgian partners have to exercise major management functions;
- the host countries' authorities must have approved the investment.

The Public Investment Corporation, SBI

The Belgian Corporation for International Investment (Société Belge d'Investissement International)(3), was set up in 1971 as a limited liability company and started operations in 1974. Out of the total capital of B.Frs.780 million, B.Frs.498 million ($13 million) had been paid up by the end of September 1981. The Government owns 58 per cent of the shares (52 per cent by the Société Nationale d'Investissement, SNI, and 6 per cent by the National Bank of Belgium). The balance is distributed among private banks and industrial firms.

The role of the SBI is to participate in the capital financing of foreign business ventures, primarily by holding equity shares or convertible debentures, and long-term convertible loans. The corporation may also provide Belgian companies with part of the capital required for foreign investment. In addition, it plays an advisory role for investment projects abroad.

SBI's activities are directed towards ventures being initiated or developed in the mutual interest of foreign countries and Belgium by the expansion of their reciprocal economic relations. Its activities are not restricted to any specific geographical area. SBI's financial involvement is necessarily complementary; when it takes the form of equity capital, this generally consists of a minority holding. Although not restricted to developing countries in its activities, the SBI views with particular interest operations reflecting the economic objectives of those countries. The involvement of local partners and business development groups, as well as international and local public institutions, is sought and welcomed by the corporation.

An analysis of the geographical and sectoral distribution of the 104 projects submitted to SBI in 1980/81 reveals a certain consistency in the orientation of

---

3. SBI, Rue Montoyer, 63, B-1040 Brussels, Telephone (02) 230 2785, Telegraphic address: Investbel, Brussels, Telex 25744 SNIM attention SBI.

Belgian investment abroad. With regard to geographical distribution, Europe and sub-Saharian Africa remain in first position, followed by Latin America and North Africa. The small proportion of projects submitted for North America is not indicative, as the type of enterprise which invests predominantly in that part of the world seldom resorts to SBI financing. On the other hand, Belgian enterprises have only limited interests in commercial or industrial implantations in South-East Asia, a region of strong economic growth. From a sectoral point of view few changes have taken place. Metal fabricates and agro-industry remain the most prominent sectors, followed in virtually identical proportion by services, textiles and leather, construction material and enterprises, chemicals and chemical engineering.

As of 30th September 1981, the end of the financial year, total investments committed by the SBI for 50 projects amounted to B.Frs.609 million ($16 million). With the addition of 3 operations authorised by the board but not yet legally undertaken, SBI's actual and potential investments as of that date amounted to B.Frs.684 million ($18 million) spread over 53 operations. The 32 investments committed or authorised in developing countries represent some 63 per cent of the total committed and authorised. If SBI investments in Belgian firms wherein study, training and management services are directed towards the developing world are included, the number rises to 38 and the corresponding percentage to 70 per cent. Total investment committed or to be committed to SBI-supported projects in developing countries approaches B.Frs.7.7 billion ($207 million). On 30th September, 1981 the SBI investment portfolio stood at B.Frs.390 million ($10 million), 40 per cent of which was held in equity, the balance consisting of long and medium-term loans.

The favourable impact of SBI's operations on the Belgian economy and employment is a consideration taken into account by SBI's management. This criterion can entail, for example, exports of equipment, spare-parts, semi-finished products, technology, know-how and services, imports of raw materials or semi-finished products needed by the Belgian industry, or the acquisition of commercial positions in foreign markets. Although it is virtually impossible to quantify the favourable impact of SBI's operations, an impression is obtained by a comparison between the sums invested by SBI and the exports of goods and services made possible for Belgian enterprises as a result:

Figures cumulated at end of financial year (in millions of B.Frs.)	80/81	79/80	78/79	77/78	76/77
Total cost of projects committed	6,786	8,064	6,464	4,491	3,742
SBI's investments	609	634	580	435	264
Related Belgian exports	9,191	11,252	10,080	7,743	5,430

Other Official Support

The General Administration for Development Co-operation regularly entrusts feasibility studies to research institutions for the benefit of developing countries and in agreement with them. Occasionally it asks Belgian firms to set up pilot industrial units or to manage vocational training centres. Technical assistance for the management of a number of enterprises is given by Belgian centres or firms under contracts with the Administration (and in compliance with the Belgian regulations governing the activities of the public sector).

4. CANADA

Exhange Control

Canada does not regulate outward direct investment transactions or transfers.

Bilateral Investment Protection Agreements

To date, Canada has not formalised any bilateral agreements with developing countries for the protection of foreign direct investment.

Investment Guarantee Scheme

The Export Development Corporation(1) provides guarantees against the three main political risks for Canadian foreign direct investment in developing countries. The maximum period of coverage is fifteen years at a premium of 1.0 per cent p.a. of the value of the original investment for the three risks combined. To be eligible, the investment must provide economic benefits to Canada and have the approval of the authorities of the host country. The investment can be in the form of equity, loans, tangible assets, management or technical service contracts, royalties, trademarks, or equipment leases. For equity and loan investment the maximum coverage for each project will be up to 100 per cent of the initial investment. In addition, 50 per cent of this amount can be covered for the reinvestment of retained earnings.

At the end of 1981, total investments in developing countries under cover had reached $105 million. In particular, small businesses continue to find the facility of great assistance in establishing abroad. Investments in 21 developing countries have been covered, with Latin America representing the region of greatest activity. The most important industrial sectors are agro-industry,

---

1. EDC, 110 O'Connor Street, Box 655, Ottawa, Ontario K1P ST9, Canada, Telephone: (613)2372570; Telex: 053-4136; Cable: EXCREDCORP.

pharmaceuticals, secondary manufacturing and primary resource development. The EDC also insures Canadian investment in the field of offshore oil exploration and development.

Fiscal Measures

The Canadian Income Tax Act does not make a distinction between income from investments in developing countries and those made in other countries. However, tax-sparing is granted under the provisions of specific double taxation conventions with developing countries. The most important measures available to Canadian investors are as follows:

 i) Taxes on income or profit paid in the source country generally are eligible for credit against Canadian income taxes payable, this credit being limited to the amounts of Canadian taxes otherwise payable on such income;

 ii) Canada has double taxation conventions in force with several developing countries. These conventions not only provide for specific mechanisms to avoid double taxation, normally by way of a credit, but also reduce, and put a ceiling on, the rate of withholding tax that may be imposed on dividends, interest and royalties paid by a resident of one country to a resident of the other. In addition, Canadian residents are generally granted a credit for certain taxes which have not been paid if they fall within those specified in the conventions, e.g. a tax holiday granted by the developing country;

 iii) Business earnings of a subsidiary of a Canadian company are not subject to Canadian tax if the subsidiary is not incorporated in Canada (i.e. is not "resident"). A resident corporation is taxable in Canada, and a credit is granted for foreign taxes;

 iv) Dividends received by a Canadian company from a foreign affiliate in which it has at least 10 per cent control are taxable in Canada. Relief from double taxation is provided by a credit for the foreign withholding tax. However, when a double taxation convention is in force, the dividends are exempt from corporate tax in Canada.

Other Official Support

Authorised in September 1978, the Industrial Co-operation Program is an extremely complex but flexible policy instrument based on mutual benefit using financial incentives to mobilise outside resources for development, usually via technology transfer or technical assistance. It is the Aid-Trade Interface.

Through the Program, contributions to Canadian companies reduce the risk costs of investigating joint ventures, licensing arrangements, long-term management contracts, co-production agreements and other forms of co-operation in the Third World; allow developing country counterparts to visit Canada and provide for the training of key personnel and for other similar activities. The testing and adapting of Canadian technology to local conditions is provided for by contributions under the Canadian Transfer Facility; for Canadian manufacturers in the field of renewable energy, to test and adapt their technology in developing countries as a prelude to technology transfer. Canadian institutions and business associations may receive contribution for studies, seminars, and workshops, for training and for technical assistance projects. Missions to and from Canada to bring potential partners together are an ongoing function of the Program, as is information dissemination through the provision worldwide of Canadian business and technical periodicals, or via commissioned studies in Canada and in the Third World. Direct technical co-operation through both Canadian and Third World organisations is funded under the umbrella of the Program. Financial assistance to perform pre-feasibility studies for large capital projects is provided to Canadian consultants via the Canadian Project Preparation Facility when these are required by developing countries as a prerequisite to multilateral or bilateral financing. Long-term industrial contributions are also available to developing country governments so that they may have access to Canadian experts and expertise in developing and implementing their industrialisation programmes, in strengthening their institutions, and in analysing and delineating policy priorities for economic growth.

The Industrial Co-operation Division of the Canadian International Development Agency (CIDA) stimulates and responds to requests for assistance by judging projects against criteria established for each Program element. The process involves analysis of the potential benefits to the developing country and to Canada; assessment of the chances of success; evaluation of the applicant's capacity to implement; negotiation of the level of assistance to be provided; and a decision on as to whether to proceed. It involves detailed discussions with the applicant, and consultations within the interdepartmental community, with the Canadian diplomatic mission(s) concerned, and, often, the local diplomatic mission and regional financial institutions. Costs range from a few thousand to millions of dollars, and because the nature of projects handled varies greatly, each must be treated as unique and be examined on its individual merits.

5. DENMARK

Exchange Control

Transactions for direct investment abroad require a licence from the Danish National Bank which is usually granted. Transactions for equity investment of less than D.Kr.500,000 ($71,400) per year are exempt from licencing.

Bilateral Investment Protection Agreements

So far, Denmark has concluded bilateral agreements for the protection of direct investments with Malawi, Indonesia, and Romania.

Investment Guarantee Scheme

The Danish investment guarantee scheme, which was established in 1966, is administered by the Danish International Development Agency (DANIDA)(1) in the Ministry of Foreign Affairs. The scheme provides coverage for the three main political risks for new direct investment in developing countries. In principle, the scheme applies only to those investments which give the investor a certain degree of control over an enterprise. Portfolio investments are therefore excluded although long-term loans of an investment-like character may be covered. Only investments which have a positive developmental effect on the economy of the host country are eligible. Investment guarantees are available for private commercial and industrial enterprises with registered offices in Denmark. The investor bears 10 or 15 per cent of the risk himself depending on the existence of an investment protection agreement with the host country. The guarantee covers both the initial investment and earnings up to 8 per cent p.a. for up to three years. The maximum duration of the insurance is 15 years. Only coverage of the three risks combined is available at a premium of 0.5 per cent p.a. At the end of 1981, policies issued represented total liabilities of DK 189 million ($27 million).

---

1. DANIDA, 2 Asiatisk Plads, DK-1448 Copenhagen K. Telephone 01-920000, Telex 31292 etr DK.

The Public Investment Corporation, IFU

The Industrialisation Fund for Developing Countries(2) was established by Act of Parliament in 1967 as a non-profit autonomous institution, based on the same principles as the British CDC and the German DEG. Operations started in 1968 with the purpose of promoting investments in developing countries in co-operation with private Danish industry and, whenever possible, local investors. Although it is not required that the Danish partner control the enterprise, he should at least have a substantial influence on the company's management as long as the IFU is a partner. Economically viable joint ventures which are approved by the host country are eligible for cofinancing in all non-European developing countries, Malta and Turkey.

The IFU not only provides equity and loan financing but also feasibility studies, the transfer of know-how and other services. As a rule, IFU's participation is limited to 35 per cent of the share and loan capital and will not exceed the Danish partner's holdings, although exceptions to this rule may be made for investments in the least developed countries. However, the IFU does not seek managerial responsibilities in joint ventures.

As regards sectors of activity, IFU concentrates on manufacturing and agro-business and also on such sectors as tourism, industrialised housing, consulting engineering and transportation, including local shipping. It does not, however, participate in trading companies. Its financial assistance is not tied to the purchase of Danish equipment. The IFU will withdraw from a project when the enterprise has reached economic stability, usually after six to eight years of operation. Its partners in the enterprise have a priority right to acquire IFU's share.

The resources of IFU are supplied by the government. Its total assets, including retained earnings, amounted to DK 673 million ($96 million) at the end of 1981. IFU had participated or was participating in 62 projects, representing cumulative commitments of DK 360 million ($51 million).

---

2. IFU, 4 Bremerholm, DK-1069 Copenhagen K. Tel. 01-142575, Telex: 15493 IFU DK.

6. FINLAND

Exchange Control

Direct investment abroad by Finnish residents requires individual authorisation from the Bank of Finland in its capacity as exchange control authority. No other ministries or official bodies are concerned except in the case of commercial banks, which may invest in foreign shares only with the approval of the Government. The main principle applied in the current balance of payments situation is that a direct investment abroad should promote exports or otherwise be favourable from a balance of payments point of view. Investments by sales companies with the marketing of Finnish products or services as their main purpose are freely authorised, provided the amounts transferred do not exceed FIM 1 million ($232,000) per year.

Investment Protection Agreements

To date, a bilateral agreement for the protection of private investments has been signed with the Arab Republic of Egypt.

Investment Guarantee Scheme

The Finnish investment guarantee scheme, which came into operation in February 1981, is administered by the Export Guarantee Board (Vientitakuulaitos, VTL)(1) and is in principle available for investments in all developing countries on the DAC-list. It provides a guarantee against the three main categories of political risks: expropriation, war and restrictions on remittances. All companies and institutions based in Finland are eligible for investment guarantees provided they can be expected to carry out the investment successfully. The investment may be in the form of an equity participation in a foreign enterprise or of loans or guarantees of loans to such an enterprise. Reinvested earnings also may be

---

1. VTL, Eteläranta 6, P.O. Box 187, SF-00131 Helsinki 13, Telephone: 661811, Telex: 121778 vtl sf.

covered to the extent that such earnings at the time of
reinvestment are freely transferable to Finland. Coverage can also be given for remitted earnings up to 8 per
cent p.a. The maximum period of coverage is 20 years.

To qualify for insurance the investor must intend to
keep his investment for at least three years. The investor is also required to demonstrate that his project
will provide economic benefits to both Finland and the
host country. The investment must always receive the
approval of the local government. Coverage will be provided only for projects which represent new investments
or considerable expansions, modernisations or improve-
ments of existing investments. The policy always covers
all three risk categories, the annual premium for capital
investment being 0.5 per cent and for remitted earnings
0.7 per cent. The maximum percentage of cover is 90 per
cent. VTL's liability ceiling for the investment guarantee scheme is FIM 400 million ($93 million).

Fiscal Measures

Finland applies the same taxes on the net income of
foreign and domestic operations. However, dividends,
interest and royalties - other than paid from Finland and
effectively connected with a foreign branch company in
Finland - are taxed at the source on a gross income
basis. Unless a double taxation agreement applies,
foreign national income taxes on foreign source income
may be credited against Finnish state (national) income
tax on the foreign source income. Depreciation allowances for tax purposes are the same for domestic and
foreign operations. To promote the activities of Finnish
industry in developing countries, agreements for the
avoidance of double taxation have been concluded with
Brazil, India, Israel, the Republic of Korea, Morocco,
the Philippines, Singapore, Tanzania, Zambia(2) and the
Arab Republic of Egypt. As a general rule these treaties
provide for a proportionally higher taxation in the country where an investment has been made than do tax agreements between Finland and developed countries. Under a
treaty a Finnish company will commonly be exempt from a
domestic tax on dividends from a foreign subsidiary and
also when the "exemption" method is applied for avoiding
double taxation on income from a foreign branch. On the
other hand, where the "tax credit" method is used (as a
general method or in relation to certain items of income)
Finland has agreed to a credit for taxes spared in recognition of the incentives granted by the contracting
country.

---

2. Not yet in force.

The Public Investment Corporation, FINNFUND

The Finnish Fund for Industrial Development Co-operation Ltd. FINNFUND(3) was established by the Finnish Government in 1979. The Fund, which became operational in 1980, is a joint stock company with a capital of 80 million Finnish marks (some $20 million) of which the Government's share is 90 per cent. The rest of the shares are held by the Finnish Export Credit Ltd., the Industrialisation Fund of Finland Ltd., and the Confederation of Finnish Industries. The Fund is subordinated to the Ministry of Foreign Affairs. On its Board of Directors the following Ministries and institutions are represented: the Department for International Development and Co-operation in the Ministry for Foreign Affairs (FINNIDA), the Ministry of Trade and Industry, the Ministry of Finance, the Department for Foreign Trade in the Ministry for Foreign Affairs, the Finnish Export Credit Ltd. and the Industrialisation Fund of Finland Ltd.

Investment of government funds through FINNFUND are made on terms qualified as official development assistance. The purpose of FINNFUND is to contribute to the economic and social development in developing countries through participation in their industrialisation efforts. The Fund promotes the initiation, establishment and expansion of joint venture enterprises in developing countries, in co-operation with local and Finnish entrepreneurs. Although the operations of FINNFUND shall cover their own costs, the Fund's activities are in line with the Finnish development aid programme, e.g. using United Nation's definitions for the selection of beneficiary countries and taking into account the special needs of the least developed countries. Loans granted by FINNFUND are normally in Finnish marks and are freely convertible. Loans of up to 10 years maturity normally have a grace period of two years and an interest rate of 4 per cent. It is assumed that the share of investment which is denominated in local currency is financed by borrowing on the local financial market and through local equity participation. In 1981, the Fund entered into new commitments for equity investment of $3.4 million and for ODA loans of $3.4 million.

The choice of partners is determined by the Fund's aim of combining the efforts of Finnish entrepreneurs and its own resources on the one hand, with the local resources of the host country on the other. The Fund will assist in particular medium and small-scale industrial companies. The Finnish partner is expected to provide technical and managerial know-how on a long-term

----

3. FINNFUND, Unioninkatu 30, P.O. Box 237, SF-00171, Helsinki 17. Telephone (90) 171202. Telex 125028. Ffund sf.

basis. The local partner is expected to contribute local know-how and equity. To be eligible a project should be a profitable enterprise in the industrial sector which fits into the host country's development plan. Approval of the project by the host country's Government is therefore required.

If FINNFUND acquires shares in a joint venture in a developing country, it is usually a minority participation which corresponds in size to that of the Finnish partner. A typical pattern is 20 per cent for the latter two and 60 per cent for the partner in the host country. Once the joint venture is operating on a self-sustaining basis, the mission of the Fund is considered completed and its shares may be offered to the other counterparts. FINNFUND usually reserves the right to nominate a member to the Board of Directors of the enterprise. In specific cases FINNFUND can participate in the financial arrangements led by a local development finance institution or investment bank. The Fund may also acquire shares in these institutions.

Other Official Support

FINNFUND also participates in financing costs of project preparation work and feasibility studies. In general, the firm's financing share should be at least 50 per cent of the cost of the study. Financing is provided to the project on a risk basis, with a possible repayment obligation of FINNFUND's share. If the preparatory study leads to the establishment of a joint venture, the costs of study are charged to the project.

7. FRANCE

Exchange Control

The legal and administrative treatment of French outward direct investment differs as between the Franc Area countries(1) and other countries:

a) French residents are free to invest in the Franc Area without prior authorisation. Guaranteed convertibility of currency is one of the most powerful incentives to private investment, and from this point of view the structure of the Franc Area provides effective encouragement. The currencies issued by the Central Bank of the Central African States(2) and by the Central Bank of the West African States(3) are defined in terms of the French franc and guaranteed by the French Treasury. Transfers are therefore not only free inside the Franc Area, but also benefit from an exchange guarantee.

b) Direct investment transfers to EEC member countries require prior notification to the Ministry of Economics.

c) Direct investment transfers exceeding FFrs.1 million per year to other countries require official authorisation and have to be financed from foreign sources.

---

1. In January 1982 the following countries belonged to the Franc Area: France, The French Overseas Departments (Guadaloupe, Guyana, Martinique, Réunion), the French Overseas Territories (Mayotte, New Caledonia, Wallis and Futuna, St. Pierre and Miquelon, French Polynesia), Cameroon, Central African Republic, Chad, Comoros, Congo (People's Republic of), Benin, Gabon, Ivory Coast, Mali, Niger, Senegal, Togo, Upper Volta.
2. Cameroon, Central African Republic, Chad, Congo and Gabon.
3. Benin, Ivory Cost, Niger, Senegal, Togo and Upper Volta.

Bilateral Investment Protection Agreements

A Multilateral Convention on the Fundamental Rights of Nationals was signed in 1960 between France, Senegal, Madagascar, the Central African Republic, Congo (People's Republic of), Chad, and Gabon. This agreement is supplemented by bilateral conventions. A Convention of Establishment was signed with Togo in 1963 and a Co-operation Agreement with Mali in 1962.

Bilateral agreements on investment protection have been signed with the following countries: Tunisia, Zaire, Mauritius, Indonesia, Haiti, Yugoslavia, Egypt, South Korea, Malaysia, Morocco, Singapore, Philippines, Malta, Romania, Jordan, Syria, Sudan, Paraguay, Liberia, Sri Lanka. Negotiations are in progress with several other countries.

Investment Guarantee Scheme

As an incentive to set up establishments which are of definite benefit to the French economy, the Ministry for Economics and Finance operates a system of official guarantees against political risks. Applications are considered and decided upon individually, and it is essential that the operations to which they relate should not already have been carried out. The guarantee system consists of two distinct procedures:

- the first, managed by the BFCE(4), is a general scheme designed to encourage the growth of French industrial establishments, services and know-how abroad. Guarantees are given contingent upon the results of an analysis of the justification of the project and its various direct and indirect consequences for the French economy, usually on the assumption of a long-term involvement of the French investor;
- the other, managed by COFACE(5), is designed to encourage so-called "export-generating" investments, i.e. those which rapidly bring about a significant increase in exports of French goods or services. Its provisions are more advantageous, but they are contingent upon the investors' commitment to an export programme, with the application of a scale of penalties if not carried out.

---

4. Banque Française du Commerce Extérieur, 21, Boulevard Haussmann, 75009 Paris. Telephone: 247 47 47, Telex: B.F.C.E. 660370F.
5. Compagnie Française d'Assurance pour le Commerce Extérieur, 32, rue Marbeuf, 75008 Paris. Telephone: 256 60 20, Telex: 650342 asexp.

The two schemes are legally similar but differ significantly in the criteria on which the guarantees are given, and in the levels of cost and coverage. At the end of 1981 the total amount of investment covered was $378 million, of which BFCE held $260 million and COFACE $118 million.

The following features are common to both schemes:

a) BFCE and COFACE act as managers on behalf of the French government.
b) Guarantees are extended on a case to case basis, considering the benefit of each investment project to the French economy, decided by the Minister for Economics and Finance on the advice of an inter-Ministerial body.
c) Only new investments, i.e. those not yet completed when the application is made, can qualify.
d) The notion of new investment includes the creation of a production potential, the expansion of an existing one, or a new participation in an existing enterprise.
e) Detailed conditions for the guarantees and the rules governing their implementation are laid down once and for all at the outset for a fixed period (though there may be a review of a project which has meanwhile developed).
f) Guarantees are expressed in French francs on the basis of the amount transferred at the time the investment is made (amounts in foreign currencies are converted into francs at the rates ruling on the date of the transfer). The coverage is therefore related not to the value of assets held abroad but to the amount of capital committed. Indemnification in case of loss may not, however, exceed the net asset value of the investment as it was before the events occurred which gave rise to the claim.
g) Transfers may be made in cash or in kind under certain conditions.
h) Transfers covered are usually those made for the purpose of subscribing capital. But by extension guarantees may also apply to issue premiums, blocked accounts and long-term loans by shareholders, payments to a branch or agency, or guarantees given by investors to cover long-term loans by third parties insofar as such financing or undertakings are in the nature of the investment, a question which is decided in each individual case.
i) Guarantees become effective immediately after the related transfers are made.
j) Within limits profits reinvested or eligible for repatriation may be covered.
k) Investors must be French. This does not

necessarily mean that an enterprise is not eligible for a guarantee if a part of its capital is owned by an individual or firm from a third country. Enquiries will be made, in particular, into their status as principals.

1) Guarantees relate only to claims arising directly out of political acts. Insofar as they are the direct consequence of such acts claims are met when any of the following risks materialises:

   - Interference with property: impossibility of exercising rights attaching to the investment, destruction or reduction in value of the assets of the foreign enterprise, impossibility of conducting its business normally;
   - Non-payment: impossibility of obtaining payment for ceding the investment, for liquidation, compensation in case of expropriation, or for any dividends covered;
   - Non-transfer: impossibility of transferring outside the country the amounts due as above.

The special features of the scheme managed by BFCE are as follows:

a) Applications for guarantees require a decision by the Minister for Economics and Finance on the advice of a specialised inter-Ministerial committee under the chairmanship of the Director of the Treasury, known as the Grants Committee for Treasury Guarantees for French Investments Abroad (Comité d'octroi de la garantie du Trésor aux investissements français à l'étranger). The files have to be deposited with the BFCE which investigates them and issues and manages guarantees that have been approved. The guarantees are in the material form of a "Contrat de Garantie" signed between BFCE and the investor.

b) The operation must be of benefit to the French economy. This benefit is appraised on the basis of the direct and indirect effects shown by an analysis through time of the submitted investment programme. The appraisal is not only in terms of immediate activity but may also take account of the international dimension which the planned establishment can secure for the French enterprise concerned, and of its contribution to spreading the reputation of French techniques throughout the world. Conversely, an investment with no noteworthy positive effect on the French economy cannot receive a guarantee.

c) The investment must be approved by the authorities of the foreign country which may have secured an agreement with France on the protection of investments or be linked with the French Treasury by an operations account (African

Franc Area). A number of other countries are also eligible by derogation(6).

d) Guarantees may be given to direct investments in almost all sectors: manufacturing industry, engineering, services (insurance, transport, tourism) marketing, and so on. They are refused in principle for the following sectors:

- oil prospection (though they may be granted for the development of oil fields and to petro-industries);
- agriculture (though they may be granted for industries processing or marketing agricultural products);
- real estate (though they may be granted for hotel investments);
- financial holdings (though they may be granted for participations of financial institutions when they serve as substitute for the industrial investors);

e) Indirect investment through a holding company or temporary bridging operations carried out by a financial institution on account of the principal investor can also be covered.

f) Detailed conditions for the guarantee are fixed in each case by the Director of the Treasury on the advice of the Grants Committee. In principle there is no lower or upper limit to the percentage or amount of participation in the foreign enterprise. The Committee appraises the nature and advisability of the investment mainly from the standpoint of the control which it gives the French investor over the activities of the subsidiary. Investments which are made before an application file is lodged with BFCE, or which are to finance the participation of a local associate, do not in principle qualify for guarantees. Guarantees may be extended, on a case-by-case basis, to profits for reinvestment (capitalisation) or for repatriation (dividends) with cumulative limits of 50 per cent and 25 per cent of the initial investment respectively. The application for a guarantee must be made before the amounts are allocated, and must accompany the original application.

g) The fraction guaranteed, i.e. the percentage of the loss which is indemnified in the event of a claim, is normally 90 per cent. The Committee may, however, fix lower fractions, depending on the details of the file. In some cases, for investments of exceptional interest to the French

6. For bilateral agreements see page 60; for the franc area see page 59.

economy, the fraction may be higher, though it may not exceed 95 per cent. The investor must not obtain other guarantees for the remaining percentage of uncovered risk.

h) Guarantees take effect from the time at which the related transfers are made. The duration of a guarantee is decided by the Committee according to the characteristics of the investment, in particular its economic depreciation. It may not exceed 15 years. Where an investment is carried out over a period of time, however, the starting date for measuring the duration may be the mid-point of the transfers, provided that the total duration does not exceed 17 years.

i) There is no scaling-down of the amounts guaranteed in the last years of the guarantee period in countries which have agreed upon an investment protection convention with France or are linked with the French Treasury by an operations account. In the case of investments in countries which are eligible by derogation, however, the maximum amount guaranteed in each of the last three years of the period is in principle reduced to 75 per cent, 66 per cent and 50 per cent respectively, of the amount initially covered.

j) The commission payable annually in advance by the beneficiary for a guarantee is calculated on the basis of the capital sum invested and guaranteed (after deduction of the non-guaranteed percentage). The annual rate is normally 0.7 per cent for investments covered by an investment protection convention between the foreign country and France or made in countries linked with the French Treasury by an operations account. It is between 0.8 per cent and 0.9 per cent in other cases, depending on the degree of protection given to the investment by the authorities of the foreign country. In exceptional cases it may be as high as 1 per cent (a distinction being made, in particular, between investments covered by a national investment code or other favourable unilateral provisions). If an investment is of particular interest for French exports but does not meet the conditions required for eligibility to the COFACE scheme described below, all or part of the provisions applying to "export-generating" investments may be applied.

k) In the event of a claim, the beneficiary is indemnified if the risk was the direct consequence of one of the following acts:

- measures taken by the foreign authorities with the deliberate intention to prejudice the investor's interests because of his nationality;
- an act or decision of the foreign authorities

(nationalisation, expropriation, confiscation, sequestration);
- violation by those authorities of any specific actions by them concerning the investment (acts recognised only within the limits fixed in each case);
- war, civil war, revolution or rioting in the foreign country;
- general moratorium declared by the foreign authorities;
- political events or economic difficulties arising, or legislative or administrative measures taken, outside France resulting in non-transferability.

1) Industrial investments in the mining sector may benefit from more favourable conditions:

- application may be considered for any country, and it has already been indicated that OECD countries are eligible;
- the percentage of cover may be 95 per cent;
- the duration may be of 20 years;
- there is no scaling down of the guarantee, for any country;
- the commission, settled according to the risk, is as moderate as possible in the normal range.

Generally speaking, applications concerning mining investments are investigated in a flexible way, in order to find solutions adapted to their specificity.

The special features of the scheme for "export-generating investments" managed by COFACE are described below:

a) Applications for guarantees are submitted for decision by the Minister for Economics and Finance on the advice of the Commission des Garanties et du Crédit au Commerce Extérieur ("Guarantees Committee") under the chairmanship of the Director of External Economic Relations (Direction des Relations Economiques Extérieures). Files have to be submitted by investors with the COFACE which investigates them and issues and manages the guarantees resulting from a favourable decision. These guarantees are in the form of an insurance policy signed between COFACE and the investor.
b) The applicant must be able to demonstrate that the planned investment will bring about an increase in French exports in a way corresponding to one of the three following cases (multiplying factors):

First case: The operation results in a net current flow of additional French exports (compared
with those which could normally be expected if
the investment had not been made) totalling at
least 3.5 times the amount of the initial capital
transfers for the investment to be guaranteed,
during the first five years following the date of
the investment. This current flow must not include supplies and equipment needed for the local
physical investment, and it is taken at its net
value, i.e. less any additional imports into
France resulting from the operation. Exports may
be excluded if the greater part of their value
consists of imports.

Second case: The basic supplies and services of
French origin required to carry out the local
physical investment represent at least 6.7 times
the amount of the initial capital transfers for
the investment to be guaranteed (i.e. the amount
of the initial transfers to be guaranteed does
not exceed 15 per cent of the amount of the exports resulting from the investment).

Third case: The operation is not eligible in
accordance with either of the two cases above,
but the cumulative total of the two types of exports (initial supplies to carry out the local
physical investment, plus the net current flow)
over the first five years exceeds eight times the
amount of the initial capital transfers for the
investment to be guaranteed.
If the operation is carried out by several French
investors acting in common, the transfers taken
into account in these calculations are in principle those made with respect to the total initial
French share in the investment. There is no geographical restriction save in exceptional circumstances, and all investments of whatever kind are
eligible if they meet the conditions laid down on
the matter of their link with exports.
c) Details and conditions for the guarantee are
fixed in each case by the Director of External
Economic Relations on the advice of the Guarantees Committee, in accordance with its appraisal
in terms of the conditions for eligibility set
out above, and on the basis of the investor's
undertaking as to the export programme submitted.
d) In principle, there is no lower or upper limit to
the percentage or amount of participation in the
foreign enterprise. The essential point is that
the percentage and manner of French participation
shall ensure that the export programme as
submitted is realistic. In principle, any transfers made before the filing of the application
with COFACE do not qualify for a guarantee.

Guarantees may extend to profits for reinvestment (capitalisation) or for repatriation (dividends) within cumulative limits of 100 per cent and 50 per cent respectively of the amount of the initial investment. The application for a guarantee must be made before their allocation.

e) The fraction covered may be as high as 95 per cent depending on the characteristics of the operation. The investor must not obtain other guarantees for the remaining percentage of the risk.

f) Guarantees take effect from the time at which the related transfers are made, and their duration may not exceed 15 years. The period is measured from the date of the transfers if they are all made at the same time, or, if they are made in succession, from the date on which the total transferred reaches one-half of the planned investment. However, the duration may subsequently be extended by another five years, but no more than a total of 20 years, if the investor commits himself to an export programme during these five years which represents at least five times the initial annual export programme.

g) There is no scaling-down of the amounts guaranteed in the last few years of the guarantee period.

h) The annual premium payable, calculated on the basis of the capital sum invested and guaranteed (after deduction of the non-guaranteed percentage) is 0.4 per cent. If, however, the investment is being made in a country where there are special risks and which has not entered into an investment protection convention with France, the premium may vary between 0.5 per cent and 0.6 per cent.

i) In the event of a claim, the beneficiary is indemnified if the risk was the direct consequence of one of the acts qualifying for indemnification under the BFCE scheme, or of one of the following acts:

   - changes in the legislation of the foreign country concerning foreign investment;
   - sudden and unforseeable closing of the market of the foreign country to the exports whose expansion the investment was designed to encourage.

j) The conditions of eligibility provide that the investor must submit a proposal outlining the export impact of his investment. This programme, submitted while the application file is being examined, is then incorporated into the special conditions of the insurance policy. Supervision of its execution is accompanied by a scale of

penalties. For this purpose investment evaluation is carried out in two stages: a preliminary examination after three years, and a
decision after five years. The scale of penalties is as follows:

- If the amount of exports is not less than
  80 per cent of the forecast the guarantee is
  maintained;
- If it is between 50 per cent and 80 per cent of
  the forecast, but nonetheless enables the minimum multiplying factor to be attained, the
  amount of reinvested or repatriable profits
  guaranteed is reduced by between 25 and 50 per
  cent;
- If it is below 50 per cent of the forecast, or
  if the minimum multiplying factor cannot be
  attained, the fraction covered is reduced by
  10 per cent (12 per cent in case of claims
  arising between years 6 and 10, 15 per cent in
  case of claims arising during the first five
  years). The premium is increased to 0.9 per
  cent and the amount of reinvested or repatriable profits guaranteed is reduced by 50 per
  cent;
- If the exports taken into account do not equal
  twice the amount of the investment the guarantee is withdrawn (except in a case of exceptional circumstances or on the reasoned advice
  of the Administration).

Fiscal Measures

So far as tax incentives to investment are concerned, the relations between France and the developing
countries are such that the latter fall into five groups:

First group: Countries with which there are no tax
conventions. Straightforward application of French tax
laws, and the rules of territoriality in particular, differs for firms and individuals:

a) Profits made outside France by firms subject to
   company tax are not liable for French taxation
   when made by a subsidiary or branch established
   abroad. Losses incurred outside France in the
   same circumstances are not deductible from profits eligible for tax in France. However, French
   firms investing abroad with a view to setting up
   a sales establishment or a research or information office, either directly or through a
   subsidiary, may include among their costs deductible for tax purposes an amount equal to the
   losses suffered during the first five years of
   operation of such establishment or subsidiary, up

to the limit of the capital invested during those
years. (The deductible amount may in certain
cases equal the amount of capital invested during
the first five years.) In addition, French firms
making an industrial investment in developing
countries, either directly or through a subsidiary, may, with the approval of the Minister for
Economics and Finance, qualify for a tax-free
reserve which may not, however, exceed one-half
of the capital invested during the first five
years of operations. Deductions in these circumstances must be added in equal parts to taxable
profits during the five financial years following
the first five years of operations.
Finally, dividends distributed by foreign subsidiaries of French companies benefiting from the
tax regulations applying to the parent company
are taxable in France only for 5 per cent of
their amount.

b) Profits made by individuals or partnerships liable for personal income tax are taxable in
France, whatever the origin of the profits, so
long as such individuals or partnerships have
their residence or main place of business in
France. Profits arising abroad are taxed in
France, however, only up to the net amount of any
tax that may have been paid abroad.

The provisions for encouraging the setting up of
sales establishments or research or information offices
outside France also apply to undertakings in the form of
individuals or partnerships liable for personal income
tax.

Second group: Guinea, Vietnam, Cambodia, and Laos.
The French regulations which traditionally apply to these
countries is in the form of a system of "fiscal neut-
rality" whereby the French tax authorities allow tax on
distributed profits collected in the host countries to be
deducted from French tax payable on dividends arising in
those countries.

Third group: The French Overseas Territories, the
Black African States and Madagascar, Algeria and
Tunisia. These States are linked to France by bilateral
tax conventions designed to eliminate double taxation.
So far as income from securities is concerned these conventions provide for flat-rate tax relief varying from
country to country, increased in inverse proportion to
the amount of tax collected locally. The effect of these
incentives is to confer a yield on capital invested in
securities in those countries that is higher than would
be obtained in countries not linked to France by a tax
convention, and generally more advantageous than that
which would result from mere elimination of double
taxation.

Fourth group: Certain developing countries outside the Franc area, with which conventions of a special type have been established (Israel, India, Lebanon, Pakistan, Brazil, Iran, Singapore, Malaysia and the Philippines). As a general rule, these conventions avoid double taxation for French investors and enable them to retain the tax benefits which the States in this group allow to foreign investors, particularly with respect to income from securities (matching credit, sparing tax).

Fifth group: Special tax arrangements encourage private investment in the French Overseas Departments including the acquisition of land.

Official Financial Support for Private Investment

A. The Caisse Centrale de Coopération Economique (CCCE)(7)

Though mainly concerned with official aid, the role of the Caisse Centrale de Coopération Economique in private financing is an important one. Its direct support of French private investment mainly takes the form of medium-term rediscount credits, long-term loans and, to a very small extent, the taking of holdings in enterprises. Furthermore the CCCE works in close co-operation with development banks in developing countries. It takes holdings in the capital of these banks and makes loans to them to enable them to participate in financing local enterprise, both public and private. It plays an important part in preparing and supervising projects financed in this way.

Since 1963 the Caisse Centrale has worked out various formulas which allow a broad association of French and local private capital in financing projects. This has been achieved in particular by coupling its long-term loans either with medium-term bank credits, which are rediscountable with overseas issuing institutes or with payments facilities provided by suppliers benefiting from credit insurance. In order to allow wider recourse to medium-term bank credit, the Caisse Centrale has on various occasions agreed to allow grace periods of as much as 5 years for the repayment of its loans. A certain number of private enterprises have thus succeeded in carrying out investment projects using a financing formula consisting, besides their own funds, of about one-third long-term credits from the Caisse Centrale.

Loans by the Caisse Centrale to private enterprises

_____

7. CCCE, 233 Boulevard Saint-Germain, F-75007 Paris, Telephone: 550 32 20; Telex: 200750.

in the African and Malagasy States (EAM) are only a small part of the total funds lent by the Caisse Centrale to foreign states and go mainly to industry. In recent years the Caisse Centrale has tried to intervene for the benefit of three sectors, in particular, that are of special importance to development: food crops, agro-industry and productive capital equipment.

B. The Fund for Aid and Co-operation (FAC)

The Fonds d'Aide et de Coopération (FAC) makes grants to public or semi-public bodies to enable them to take holdings in the capital of companies contributing to the development of the African and Malagasy States (e.g. Bureau de Recherches Géologiques et Minières). FAC action in favour of private initiative also takes the form of loans for the partial financing of preinvestment studies and contributions to vocational training pro-grammes. Finally, the FAC takes direct part in the establishment of industrial units by special very long-term loans known as "second-rank loans" made to the pro-moting company. These special loans, the repayment of which is deferred until after all other lenders have been paid off, may be treated as funds owned by the enterprise concerned.

C. Union pour le financement et l'expansion du com-merce international (UFINEX)

Loans for financing investment abroad may be ob-tained from the UFINEX company which obtains its funds by means of government-guaranteed bond issues. It grants credits for maximum periods of 15 years. Approximately 25 per cent of its loans are for investments in the de-veloping countries. UFINEX only takes part in investment operations that will generate a volume of French exports three to four times greater than the initial investment, within a five-year period. The proportion lent varies between 50 and 100 per cent of the amount of the investment.

D. Développement Industriel à l'Etranger (DIE)

The Crédit National has extended loans, since 1972, in conjunction with the BFCE under what is known as the "DIE" procedure, to finance industrial and commercial investment abroad. Approximately one-half of the oper-ations concern developing countries.

Information and Promotion Programme

In 1963 the Secretariat of State for Co-operation

set up a Consultative Committee on industrialisation and equipment in the African and Malagasy States. Studies have been made under the auspices of this Committe with the participation of representatives of the public authorities concerned, overseas investors and French exporters to discover and decide on suitable measures for promoting industrial investment in the African and Malagasy States. Concerning these countries the Fund for Aid and Co-operation can bear up to 50 per cent of the cost of market research, feasibility studies and engineering surveys. Furthermore, the growing contributions of the FAC to vocational training programmes are partly designed to enable private companies to obtain the intermediate and technical management essential to the achievement of development projects.

8. GERMANY

Exchange Control

Direct investment abroad by German residents is free from restrictions but, the Bundesbank and the Federal Ministry of Economics must be notified of each transaction for statistical purposes.

Bilateral Investment Protection Agreements

By the end of 1981, Germany had negotiated, or signed, 49 treaties with developing countries. With these instruments, each contracting party encourages and protects capital investments made by firms from the other party. Foreign investors are thus guaranteed fair and equitable treatment (in particular national treatment and application of the most favoured nation clause). Their investments are protected against unjustified expropriation and in any case against expropriation without adequate and prompt compensation.

Other provisions normally contained in German investment promotion and protection treaties are:

- free transfer of the invested capital, earnings and liquidation proceeds at the current exchange rate;
- the treaty is valid for ten years but will remain in force if not revoked;
- for investments made before the date of expiry, the provisions of the treaty remain in force for a further period of twenty years.

The German business community considers these treaties and agreements as a generally useful contribution to a good investment climate, since experience has shown that countries shy away from even minor breaches of their international obligations once an agreement has been signed, in order not to lose the standing they enjoy in the international business community. The network of such treaties and agreements, several of which had been concluded by 1959 and the early 1960s, continues to expand. Recent additional treaties are with Bangladesh, Papua-New

Guinea and Somalia, all signed, but not yet ratified, in 1980 and 1981.

Investment Guarantee Scheme

German direct investments in developing countries can be protected against political risks by official guarantees issued under a scheme which was established in 1960. To be eligible for a guarantee, an investment must satisfy the following tests:

- it must be new (establishment of a venture or extension of an existing one);
- it must have positive effects both on the host country's and on Germany's economy;
- the situation for foreign investment in the host country must appear satisfactory, at the time of approval, with respect to legal protection against political risks. This is assumed to be the case in countries with which investment protection treaties or agreements have been made. No new guarantees can be approved for investment in countries where claims under the guaranteee scheme are pending.

The types of investment that can be guaranteed are (i) equity, (ii) loans provided to foreign enterprises in which the creditor also holds equity and (iii) dotation or endowment capital to overseas branches of German enterprises.

The guarantee covers the usual political risks:

- expropriation, nationalisation and similar, politically motivated official measures;
- war, revolution, etc.;
- impossibility of transferring capital and earnings.

The coverage offered by the guarantee is limited to 95 per cent. Reinvested earnings up to 100 per cent of the covered original investment may be included in the guarantee. Remitted earnings that have not yet been transferred are covered to the extent of eight per cent of the investment annually for up to three years. Guarantees last 15 years, but their duration can be extended for another five years. The costs for the German investor of the guarantee is a one-time inscription fee of between 0.05 and 0.1 per cent and an annual fee of 0.5 per cent of the guaranteed amount. New forms of foreign investment, replacing equity participation, that have been developed in the petroleum sector, e.g. service contracts and production sharing agreements, can also be protected against political risks by the German guarantee scheme. The object of this guarantee, introduced in 1977, is the contractor's claim to be refunded for exploration and development costs as well as his option of buying petroleum from wells developed by him. In these cases however, the coverage is limited, to 70 per cent of the capital amount invested.

Applications for guarantees are processed by a private corporation, Treuarbeit(1), acting on behalf of the government. After considering each project, an inter-ministerial committee composed of representatives of the Ministries for Economics, Finance, Foreign Affairs and Economic Co-operation decides whether to approve the guarantee for a given project or not. At the end of 1981, $1,102 million of capital investments in developing countries were guaranteed under the scheme.

Fiscal Measures

By the end of 1981, 29 bilateral agreements for the avoidance of double taxation have been completed or signed with developing countries. While such agreements commonly adopt the principle of residence as a basis of taxation, the German agreements with developing countries increasingly apply the principle of taxation in the source country. Thus, tax holidays or exemptions granted by a developing country as investment incentive are treated, under the agreements, as (fictitious) tax credits deductible from the investor's tax liabilities in Germany. In the absence of a double taxation agreement, a similar outcome is achieved by the provisions of the Foreign Taxation Act.

A special law on Tax Measures for Foreign Investments of German Industry, passed in 1969, is applicable to ventures in both developing and developed countries. Under certain conditions it allows the investor to create profit reducing reserves or to deduct losses incurred by his foreign venture from his domestic profits. Another special law applicable only to investments in developing countries, which existed since the early 1960s, was abolished at the end of 1981. This "Developing Country Tax Law", which was improved and refined considerably during the past years (the last time in 1979), provided the possibility for the German investor to build up profit-reducing reserves which had to be written back after a given time. The law differentiated the incentive according to the poverty of the host country and the type of project in which the investment was made. The reserve could amount to 100 per cent of the original investment if the host country belonged to the group of LLDCs A rate of 40 per cent applied to investments in all other developing countries. However, the incentives granted

---

1. Treuarbeit AG, New York Ring 13, D-2000 Hamburg 60, Telephone: (49-40)6378-1, Telex: tahh d 2174118.

under the Developing Country Tax Law eventually turned out not to have the desired impact on decisions of German investors, leading to its abolition.

The Public Investment Corporation, DEG(2)

The "Deutsche Entwicklungsgesellschaft" (German Development Company) was founded in 1962 with the aim of supporting and encouraging German entrepreneurs, in particular of medium and small scale, to establish branches or affiliates in developing countries. DEG's authorised capital, currently DM1 billion, is fully held by the Federal Government. The DEG is a non-profit making institution, but operates on normal business principles to the extent that this is compatible with its general objectives. The Federal government does not interfere with the selection of the individual projects, but is represented on the supervisory board, together with a majority of representatives from German industry. The DEG usually operates in partnership arrangements involving a German partner or a partner from another EEC country and a partner of the developing country. The Company actively seeks new investment opportunities and makes proposals to German industry and trade. It helps German firms establish local contacts and find local partners, and advises businessmen on operating conditions in developing countries. The financial contribution consists of equity participation or loans with equity features. Investments supported by the Company must benefit the economic development of the host country. Particular emphasis is laid on private investment in the form of joint ventures, tranfer of managerial and technological know-how, processing of local raw materials, improvement of balance of payments and the creation of permanent jobs. The respective projects must fit into the economic structure and development plan of the host country and must be approved by the host country government. "Co-ordinated projects" in which official aid is combined with private investment can also be supported. Twenty-three per cent of DEG funds are, at present, invested in national development institutes. The DEG thus co-operates indirectly in the financing of additional projects in various countries.

At the end of 1981 the DEG had made total commitments (net of return flows) of DM834 million for 201 companies in 64 developing countries. The total value invested in these projects by all partners amounted to DM8.8 billion ($3.9 billion).

---

2. Deutsche Gesellschaft für wirtschaftliche Zusammenarbeit (DEG), Belvedere-Strasse 40, D-5000 Köln 41, Telephone (221) 49861; Telex 8881949; Cable: deutschges koeln.

Since the leverage effect of the Company's activities depends largely on how many new projects it can help to start, the DEG is interested in terminating its participation in any given project as soon as this seems possible. In selling its participation to the partners, the Company thus obtains funds for new investments.

Other Forms of Support for Foreign Direct Investment

A financial support programme set up in 1979 to promote the establishment of German subsidiaries in developing countries (replacing the previous ERP subsidiary scheme) had provided commitments of DM107 million for 160 enterprises in 37 countries by 31st December, 1981. The official loans are extended at highly favourable terms: 15 years maturity including a 5-year grace period, 2.5 per cent interest for investments in LLDCs and 3.5 per cent in other developing countries. This programme is a useful addition to the already existing instruments for promoting the activities of the private sector in developing countries. In conjunction with official investment guarantees and DEG participation, it is helping to increase the level of investment undertaken by German enterprises, even in the higher-risk developing countries.

In view of the fact that smaller enterprises are often not well informed about the situation in developing countries, a number of investment advisory services, both official and private, provide information on investment opportunities for German industry, including general information on the investment climate, changes of legislation etc. in different developing countries. The Federal Agency for Foreign Trade Information(3), supervised by the Ministries for Economics and Foreign Affairs, is an important institution of this kind. As far as private institutions are concerned, German enterprises interested in ventures in developing countries may request information from one of the four "Ländervereine" in Hamburg (associations of trading companies, dealing with Africa, Latin America, East Asia and the Middle East, respectively), from the Association of German Industry (BDI) in Cologne or from the Confederation of German Chambers of Industry and Commerce (DIHT) in Bonn.

---

3. Bundesstelle für Aussenhandelsinformation, Am Blaubach 13, D-5000 Köln. Telephone (49-221) 2057-1.

9. ITALY

Exchange Control

No authorisation is required for outward investments
by enterprises, except by banks. For the latter, the
Italian Banking Law requires prior authorisation by the
banking authority for all participation operations, including direct investment abroad.

The transfer to finance foreign investment can be
made directly by Italian banks on the presentation of the
documents verifying the underlying transaction. The investor must deposit, for the entire duration of the investment, a lira equivalent of 50 per cent of the amount
transferred in a non-interest bearing account in the bank
making the transfer. However, exceptions to such requirements are granted by the Italian Exchange Office
and, in practice, exemption is always granted if the use-
fulness of the investment for the Italian economy can be
proved.

Bilateral Investment Protection Agreements

Italy has signed bilateral agreements for the protection of private investment with a number of developing
countries, notably the Ivory Coast, Gabon, Guinea, Malta,
Morocco, Niger and Tunisia. Trade and co-operation
agreements between Italy and some other developing countries also deal with the question of private investment.

Investment Guarantee Scheme

As of July 1979, direct investments in developing
and other countries could be guaranteed by SACE(1) (the
Special Section for Export Credit Insurance) which was
established in 1977 as an autonomous section of the
INA(2) (Istituto Nazionale delle Assicurazioni), the

---

1. SACE, Piazza Poli 36, 00100 Rome, Telephone
67381, Telex 613160 SACE 1.
2. INA, Via Salustiana 51, Rome.

National Insurance Institute. SACE has its own management and assets. But the link with INA is very close, the President of INA also being the President of SACE.

Decisions concerning terms of coverage, indemnification, etc. are taken by the Interministerial Management Committee (composed of officials of the relevant Ministries, INA and Mediocredito Centrale) which is appointed by decree by the Minister of the Treasury, in agreement with the Minister of Foreign Trade. The Committee meets each week to formulate its policy and to authorise coverage of transactions which are not delegated to the Director of SACE.

In principle resources available for payment of claims are made up of premiums and recoveries, of sums earned on investment of the Endowment fund and of reserve funds.

Guarantees can be extended for direct investments consisting of (i) the provision of capital for the procurement of raw materials or to enable the acquisition of contracts for the supply of goods and services and (ii) the provision of capital goods, of technologies, licences, patents, etc. The risks of nationalisation, expropriation without adequate indemnification, confiscation, sequestration, or other measures or actions undertaken by a foreign authority, are covered in addition to coverage against political and catastrophic circumstances which result in a loss or which definitively prevent continuance of the activity of the enterprise or the transfer of sums due to the Italian enterprise. The maximum coverage is 70 per cent of the initial investment value. The premium is 0.8 per cent p.a. of the current amount.

Fiscal Measures

There are no special fiscal incentives for private investment in developing countries which is subject to the same tax regulations as any other Italian investment abroad. However, these regulations are more favourable than those applied to domestic investment inasmuch as dividends received by a parent company from a foreign subsidiary are subject to a lower rate of tax than profits earned in Italy itself.

Other Incentives

Italian policy towards investment in developing countries is on the whole neutral. Italy does not have a public investment corporation or any other form of direct official financial support for private investment in developing countries. However, official subsidies are available to partially finance the cost of pre-investment studies.

10. <u>JAPAN</u>

Exchange Control

Outward direct investment requires a prior notification to the Minister of Finance should the amount of investment exceed Y3 million, and normally the resident is free to carry out the investment.

Bilateral Investment Protection Agreements

The first investment protection agreement between Japan and a developing country was signed with Egypt in 1977, followed by a similar agreement with Sri Lanka in 1982. Japan has also ratified treaties of friendship, commerce and navigation containing clauses on the protection of private interests (remittance of profits, confiscation of property, etc.) with a number of developing countries.

Investment Guarantee Scheme

In 1970, the Japanese Authorities instituted the Overseas Investment Insurance Scheme which merged two older (and rather inadequate) programmes into a single one while extending the scope of application. The use of the scheme by Japanese investors has since drastically increased. The scheme which was further improved in 1972, 1974 and 1981, is administered by the Ministry of International Trade and Industry (MITI).

The scheme provides coverage for the three principal categories of political risk, normally for the three risks combined. As regards the transfer risk, the impossibility of remittance must last at least two months. The scheme applies to direct investment in the form of equity, long-term loans to and a guarantee for a joint venture (five years or more) or a management-controlled enterprise, real estate, equipment etc. It can also apply to portfolio investment and long-term loans to and a guarantee for an enterprise which, although not under Japanese control, is engaged in the exploitation of mineral resources, timber and other goods to be imported by

Japan under long-term supply contracts. In this case,
the insurance also covers a non-political risk, the
"credit risk" (bankruptcy or default of the borrower for
six months or more), in addition to the political risks.

To be eligible for an insurance an investment must
be made in a new project or in the expansion of an existing enterprise. The project must have a favourable
effect on the host country and contribute to the development of Japan's international economic relations. The
investment climate in the host country is taken into consideration and the approval of the host country is requested in principle.

The scheme covers the principal (100 per cent) and
the profits (up to 10 per cent p.a. of the residual
amount of investment to a maximum of 100 per cent over
the contract life). The maximum period of coverage is
normally 15 years. In exceptional cases the interval
between the date of the investment and the date of the
start of operations may be added to that period. In the
event of loss, the claim payable is 90 per cent or 70 per
cent for the form of guarantee (80 per cent for credit
risk or 60 per cent for the form of guarantee) of the
original amount of investment, or the estimated value at
the time of the loss, whichever is the smaller. The
annual premium is 0.55 per cent for the three risks combined and 1.3 per cent if the policy also covers the
above mentioned "credit risk".

Total political risk insurance liabilities outstanding at the end of 1981 amounted to $5.8 billion.

Fiscal Measures

One of the basic rules of Japanese tax legislation
is to grant domestic and foreign investment equal treatment. In 1962 a more liberal method of calculating tax
credit on foreign sources of income was adopted and the
types of income eligible for tax credits expanded. In
1964 a system was set up for tax deferment on investments
in developing countries. This measure now applies to
investments made between 1st April, 1973 and 31st March,
1984.

Double taxation agreements and agreements to extend
tax credits have been concluded by Japan with the follow-
ing developing countries: Brazil, Egypt, India,
Indonesia, Korea, Malaysia (revised), Pakistan,
Philippines, Singapore (revised), Spain, Sri Lanka,
Thailand and Zambia.

Official Financial Support

The Japanese Government extends financial facilities

to Japanese investors mainly through the Export-Import Bank of Japan, the Overseas Economic Co-operation Fund (OECF) and the Japan International Co-operation Agency (JICA):

i) Established in 1950, the Exim Bank of Japan is a large institution with a great variety of activities. Although the main object of the Bank is to extend long and medium-term export credits in connection with Japanese capital equipment, the Bank also provides long-term funds to Japanese investors, whether they undertake their overseas business alone or jointly with local enterprises. Although this scheme for Overseas Investment Credit (OIC) applies to all foreign countries, around $400 million annually, more than half of the scheme's total operations, support investments in developing countries.

ii) Established in 1961, the OECF is an agency that primarily extends official development loans to the governments of developing countries. However, it also supplies funds in the form of long-term soft loans for projects carried out by Japanese enterprises if such projects are likely to promote economic development in the developing countries concerned. Funds are also available for pre-investment surveys. The annual amounts of investment credits extended by the OECF vary widely but do not usually exceed $100 million.

iii) The JICA was established in 1974. It is primarily the executing agency for technical co-operation but it also provides finance for projects in such fields as social development, agricultural and forestry development, and mining and manufacturing in developing countries, if such funds cannot be obtained from the Exim Bank of Japan or the OECF. In particular JICA facilitates the financing of infrastructure related to development projects undertaken by Japanese nationals, if such infrastructure also contributes to the development of the adjacent areas, as well as experimental development projects which are difficult to realise unless they are carried out in combination with technical innovation or development.

iv) In addition to the three public financial institutions mentioned above, the Japan Petroleum Development Corporation, and the Metal Mining Agency of Japan, both public corporations, supply funds for investment abroad in the field of exploration of petroleum and other important mineral resources. Finally, the Japan Overseas Development Corporation, is a semi-public corporation established in 1970 for the purpose of promoting the industrial development and trade of developing countries. It also provides financing to Japanese firms and nationals, mainly for the establishment of joint ventures in those countries, if the projects are considered to contribute to the economic development of the countries concerned.

Other Official Support

The Japanese Government subsidizes various private technical assistance activities to encourage direct investment in developing countries. For example, private organisations such as the Association for Overseas Technical Scholarships and the Japan Productivity Center are subsidized to accept trainees from developing countries. The International Management Association of Japan and the Japan Chamber of Commerce and Industry are also subsidised to cover up to 75 per cent of the expenses necessary to dispatch experts for managerial guidance and technical advice in developing countries. Subsidies are also provided to the Engineering Consulting Firms Association for its pre-investment survey activities and to other private bodies for surveys on the investment climate. In the field of agricultural investment, the government subsidizes the Overseas Agricultural Development Foundation for the training of experts.

11. NETHERLANDS

Exchange Control

Outward direct investment is free. Loans to foreign
subsidiaries exceeding FL.10 million ($4 million) per
year and per debtor are subject to prior authorisation.

Bilateral Investment Protection Agreements

The Netherlands has entered into bilateral agreements with a number of developing countries, which, among
other things, provide for the protection of private investments. Agreements of this nature have so far been
secured with Tunisia, Ivory Coast, Cameroon, Senegal,
Indonesia, Sudan, Kenya, Tanzania, Uganda(1), Malaysia,
Morocco, Republic of Korea, Yugoslavia, Egypt, Singapore,
Thailand and Sri Lanka(1).

Their main characteristics are the following: fair
and equitable treatment, most favoured nation treatment,
non-discrimination with respect to capital investments
(equal treatment with local enterprises), the right of
immediate transfer of profits and the repatriation of
invested capital; the payment of adequate, prompt and
effective compensation in the event of expropriation and
provisions for arbitration and subrogation.

Investment Guarantee Scheme

In 1969, the Dutch Parliament passed a bill introdu-
cing an official reinsurance scheme for non-commercial
risk policies contracted between investors and Dutch
banks or insurance companies designated by the Ministry
of Finance.

The official reinsurance scheme is operated by a
private credit insurance company, the "Nederlandse
Credietverzekering Maatschappij N.V." (Netherlands Credit

---

1. Not yet ratified.

Insurance Company)(2). The scheme only applies to new
direct investments in developing countries and is subject
to satisfactory procedural arrangements for dealing with
disputes. The preliminary approval of each investment by
the host country is required for the granting of individual policies. The Ministry of Finance fixed a ceiling
for the guarantees, which amounted to Fl.500 million
($200 million) at the end of 1981.

The scheme covers the three main categories of political risks and applies to both equity and loan investments. The initial amount insured is usually the amount
of investment in Dutch florins. A limit is fixed for
maximum indemnity of principal and earnings together (in
principle 150 per cent of the initial value of the investment). Untransferable earnings will be reimbursed
within the above ceiling to a maximum of 8 per cent per
annum of the original investment insured, applicable during the insurance year in which the revenue concerned was
payable.

The maximum length of a guarantee is 20 years and in
exceptional cases 25 years from the date of the insurance
policy. This length, however, cannot exceed 15 years
from the date at which the investment was completed.
After 10 years of full coverage, the guarantee is reduced
to 90 per cent in the eleventh year, 80 per cent in the
twelfth year and so forth until the fifteenth and last
year for which the coverage is 50 per cent. The purpose
of this provision is to reduce the commitments of the
Dutch government in good time but gradually enough so as
not to inconvenience the investor.

In the event of loss, at least 10 per cent would be
at the expense of the investor himself. The annual premium for the three risks together is normally 0.8 per
cent of the current amount. At the end of 1981
FL.122 million ($49 million) of investments in developing
countries were guaranteed.

Fiscal Measures

To date 10 bilateral tax agreements have been concluded with developing countries. In the absence of
bilateral tax conventions, the Dutch tax law does not
generally make any distinction in the treatment of income
from investment in developing or industrialised countries.

Under the Unilateral Decree on the Avoidance of
Double Taxation, which applies to all countries not
covered by bilateral agreements, the tax levied at the
source by developing countries on dividends, interest

---

2. NCM, Keizersgracht 271-277, 1016 ED Amsterdam,
Telephone.(020) 3202911; Telex: 11496 NCM NL.

and royalties may, as a rule, be credited against the tax levied in the Netherlands thereon. If the foreign tax cannot be fully offset against the amount of Dutch tax levied in one year, the Decree allows the balance to be offset against Dutch tax on the same type of income in the eight years following the year in which the dividends, interest and royalties were received from developing countries.

The Public Investment Corporation, FMO

In 1970, the Finance Company for Developing Countries, FMO(3), was created with the purpose of assisting the growth of the productive sector in developing countries, in particular by providing risk capital or by extending long and medium-term loans for local projects. The FMO can also procure or finance technical assistance, as well as participate in the share capital of local and regional development banks, or extend loans to these institutions. More recently, the FMO has started promoting small-scale enterprise through a new institutional set-up in co-operation with local institutions.

The FMO, a company with limited liability, has a share capital of F15.2 million (approximately $2 million fully paid-in) owned by the government (51 per cent) and by a large number of private bodies and individuals. By the end of 1981, the FMO had borrowed some Fl.118 million ($48 million) on the capital market with government guarantees. In addition, the government has provided the FMO with trust capital by extending loans or grants. FMO's total investment portfolio stood at Fl.270] million ($108 million) at the end of 1981.

Projects financed by the FMO must contribute to the economic and social development of the beneficiary countries and be economically viable. The FMO provides complementary finance in the form of loans and equity capital. But in principle it does not take a majority interest in the total capital invested by way of equity and loans. Dutch investors must preferably have a local partner in the developing country in order to qualify for FMO finance and technical assistance. Investments wholly owned by citizens of a developing country are also eligible for FMO participation.

As a rule, interest rates will be fixed according to prevailing market conditions in the developing country. In special cases concessionary terms and subsidies may be granted. Funds provided by the FMO are not tied to the procurement of Dutch equipment.

---

3. FMO, Naussaulaan 25, P.O. Box 85899, 2508 CN, The Hague, Telephone 070-614201, Telex 33042 nefmo.

Acting as a trustee for the government, the FMO has taken a participation in the share capital of, and extended loans to, four local development banks in Tanzania, Kenya, Indonesia, and Malawi. In addition, the FMO participates, at its own expense and risk, in the share capital of development banks in Botswana and Sri Lanka. The FMO's participation in the Development Bank of Rwanda has not yet been implemented. The FMO also entered into cooperation agreements for joint project-financing with two local development banks in Bangladesh and one in Pakistan.

The FMO co-operates with international financial institutions such as the IFC, the IDB and the EIB and with sister institutions in Europe (SRI, CCCE, CDC, DEG, IFU and KFW) within the informal co-operative association Interact. Co-financing within this framework enables projects to be implemented more quickly than would otherwise be the case.

12. NEW ZEALAND

Exchange Control

The transfer of funds for outward direct investment by New Zealand residents is subject to Reserve Bank approval, which favours those proposals which will lead to increased exports and otherwise benefit New Zealand's current account balance. Approval is subject to the requirement that surplus earnings, declared dividends, directors' fees and other income arising from the investment are repatriated to New Zealand, together with any surplus capital funds which may become available.

Under current exchange control policy the Reserve Bank consents to investment overseas by New Zealand residents where:

a) the funds required are borrowed outside New Zealand, either unsecured or secured against New Zealand held assets, and
b) the money is used for business purposes in the overseas country, in areas similar to the New Zealand operations.

Bilateral Investment Protection Agreements

To date New Zealand has not signed any specific agreements with developing countries for the protection of foreign direct investment.

Investment Guarantee Scheme

The New Zealand Investment Guarantee Scheme, administered by the Export Guarantee Office, EXGO(1) has provided coverage since 1973 for new equity investments in foreign enterprises against the three main political risks. It covers 90 per cent of the initial amount of investment and accumulated investment earnings up to the

---

1. EXGO, State Insurance Building, Box 5037, Wellington, Telephone: 720265; Telex: 31239 STATINS.

value of 90 per cent of the initial investment. The
premium for the three risks together is negotiated for
each contract. The maximum duration of the coverage is
15 years while the minimum is five years. The total
value of outstanding insurance policies at the end of
1981 was NZ$10.5 million ($9.1 million).

Fiscal Measures

To date, New Zealand has entered into four bilateral
agreements on the avoidance of double taxation with developing countries. These countries are the Philippines,
Fiji, Singapore and Malaysia.

Other Offical Support

The Export Suspensory Loan Scheme offers a rate of
assistance to exporters of 40 cents for each New Zealand
dollar spent on eligible promotional expenditure for market development.

Development of Investment in the South Pacific

The Pacific Islands Industrial Development Scheme
(PIIDS) was introduced at the end of 1976. The scheme
provides financial assistance and incentives for New
Zealand companies developing approved manufacturing operations and horticulture and agriculture-based ventures in
Pacific Forum Member countries with the objective of fos-
tering economic development opportunities. The qualifying countries are the Cook Islands, Kiribati, Nauru,
Niue, Papua New Guinea, Solomon Islands, Tonga, Vanuatu
and Western Samoa. An essential feature of the PIIDS is
the provision of incentives which comprise:

   a) small venture grants for up to 50 per cent of
      capital costs when qualifying assets do not
      exceed NZ$40,000;
   b) interest free suspensory loans up to 30 per cent
      of qualifying capital costs;
   c) grants of up to 50 per cent of costs incurred in
      undertaking feasibility studies, training of
      local employees and the transfer of plant and key
      personnel to the island location.

In addition to these direct incentives commercial
loan finance may also be available from the Development
Finance Corporation of New Zealand and financial assistance may be provided where insufficient local private or
government capital exists to fund the venture. There is
also a provision for special access to the New Zealand
market for goods manufactured by ventures under the
scheme. However, the South Pacific Regional Trade and

Economic Co-operation Agreement (SPARTECA) signed by Pacific Forum Member countries, including New Zealand and Australia, now provides for freer access of most goods from Pacific Island Forum Member countries to New Zealand and Australia.

13. <u>NORWAY</u>

Exchange Control

Outward direct investment is subject to prior authorisation by the Central Bank of Norway or, in the case of investment in the shipping industry, by the Ministry of Commerce and Shipping. Except for shipping investment, the authorisation is normally granted.

Bilateral Investment Protection Agreements

A bilateral agreement for the protection of private investments has been signed with Indonesia. A trade agreement with Madagascar also contains a clause for the protection of private investments.

Investment Guarantee Scheme

In 1964, the Norwegian government established a guarantee scheme for private investments abroad which is administered by the Export Credit Guarantee Institute GIEK(1), a public body. The potential investor must obtain the prior approval of NORAD, the Norwegian Agency for International Development, which advises the Guarantee Institute as to the potential economic benefit of the investment for the host country.

The scheme applies only to new direct investments and expansion programmes, in the form of both equity and loans. However, loans without equity participation are not eligible for guarantees. The three main categories of non-commercial risks are covered. A global ceiling for outstanding liabilities is presently set at N.Kr.12 billion ($2.01 billion) for the combined insurance of export credits on concessional terms and private investments in developing countries. The guarantee covers the initial investment for a maximum period of 20 years, and dividends and interest up to 8 per cent p.a.

_____

1. GIEK, Dronning Mauds gate 15, Oslo 2, Postbox 1756 Vika, Oslo 1. Telephone: 205140; Telex: 16783 GIEK.

for a maximum period of three years, or up to 24 per cent of the original investment. Reinvested earnings may be covered upon application. The maximum claim payable is 90 per cent of the insured amount which is normally reduced every year. The annual fee is 0.7 per cent of the current amount for the three risks combined.

Fiscal Measures

No special treatment is provided by the Norwegian tax legislation in favour of income from investments in developing countries. However, Norway entered into agreements in order to avoid double taxation with the following developing countries: Benin, Brazil, Egypt, India, Israel, Ivory Coast, Kenya, Malaysia, Malta, Morocco, Netherlands's Antilles, Portugal, Singapore, South Korea, Spain, Sri Lanka, Tanzania, Thailand, Trinidad and Tobago, Tunisia, Turkey and Zambia.

Other Official Support

In addition to the Investment Guarantee Scheme, NORAD provides the following incentives in order to stimulate private investment:

a) participation in the financing of pre-investment studies;
b) medium and long-term loan finance on concessional terms;
c) guarantees for loans from other sources;
d) grants or concessional finance for basic infrastructure;
e) investment guarantees.

As a precondition of support, NORAD will seek to ensure that projects meet the developmental needs of the countries concerned. Priority will be given to projects which increase and strengthen the productive capacity of the poorer developing countries, are labour intensive, utilise local raw materials, contribute to the improvement of managerial and technical skills, and have export potential. Only projects which are economically sound, financially viable, technically feasible and have a competent management will be supported.

Pre-investment studies carried out by the potential Norwegian investor can be supported on a reimbursable basis. NORAD may finance up to 50 per cent of eligible expenses and fees. Funds provided by NORAD are repayable if the project is implemented. In considering an application under this programme, NORAD examines resources (financial, managerial, personnel, technical, etc.) of the applicant which are needed for carrying out the overseas project, as well as his record of business achievement in Norway in similar types of projects.

NORAD can provide medium and long-term loan finance on concessional terms, i.e. with a grant element of 25 per cent (as calculated by OECD). Equity finance cannot be provided except in certain cases where loans are given to the host government or other public authorities or institutions to finance their part of the project. NORAD will not normally finance or otherwise commit itself to any enterprise for more than 50 per cent of the project's debt financing or 50 per cent of the project's total capital (including permanent working capital).

NORAD's lending decisions will be based on appraisal methods that take into account the total financial requirements of the project and the soundness of the resulting financial structure of the enterprise. Conditions for each loan with regard to collateral, reporting and performance will be agreed on an individual basis. Loans will normally be secured by a mortgage if permitted by the law of the host country, and NORAD will, as far as possible, require that loans are guaranteed by the host country's government.

NORAD can guarantee loans from other sources in cases where it has proved difficult or impossible to obtain part of the basic debt financing from commercial sources. No commission will be charged for such guarantees. Exposure limits and conditions are the same as for medium and long-term loans.

When a project is located in less developed areas where the national or local authorities are unable to finance the basic infrastructure required for project implementation, NORAD can assist with loans on concessional terms or grants. Road construction, quay and harbour development, local power distribution, housing, educational institutions and health services may qualify for support. The amount of investment required, however, should not be disproportionate in relation to the size of the overall project while it should also be readily identifiable as a sub-project. Support will usually be given on condition that local bodies be able to take over responsibility for the running of the relevant project as soon as possible.

14. SWEDEN

Exchange Control

Direct investment abroad by Swedish residents requires individual authorisation from the Riksbank (Bank of Sweden). The authorisation is granted on condition that the investment is financed by borrowing abroad of an average maturity of not less than five years. Three categories of outward direct investment are exempted from this requirement: investment in sales companies, investment in small amounts (not exceeding S.Kr.1 million) and investment in those developing countries which are the main recipients of Swedish official development assistance. The requirement of foreign borrowing can be waived also in other cases, e.g. for investments in other Nordic countries.

Bilateral Investment Protection Agreements

So far, Sweden has concluded bilateral investment protection agreements with six developing countries, namely, China, Egypt, Malaysia, Pakistan, Sri Lanka and Yugoslavia. At present (September 1982) negotiations are being held with four other countries.

Investment Guarantee Scheme

In 1968, the Swedish Parliament approved the investment guarantee scheme and charged the Swedish Export Credits Guarantee Board (Export-Kreditnämnden, EKN)[1] with its administration. Investment guarantees may be issued up to a maximum amount of S.Kr.400 million ($65 million). The scheme is primarily intended to encourage projects which benefit developing countries. Therefore it applies strict eligibility criteria concerning the contribution to the economic and social development of the host countries. For example the host

---

1. Exportkreditnämnden (EKN), Norrlandsgatan 15, P.B. 7334, 10390 Stockholm, Telephone: (08)235830; Telex: 17657.

government has to confirm the economic priority of a project. To be eligible for a guarantee, the investment should also have a positive impact on the Swedish economy.

Guarantees are only available for investment in countries which are major recipients of Swedish official development assistance, the so-called programme countries, and in other developing countries which pursue a development policy which is in line with the principals guiding Sweden's development co-operation programme. The geographical coverage of the schemes has been gradually adapted to changes in the geographical distribution of the Swedish Assistance Programme. Both new projects and expansion of existing facilities are considered for guarantees, but only direct investment which gives the investor substantial control of an enterprise, either through equity participation or loans, are eligible. Minority equity participation is examined on a case by case basis. Financial participations as well as contributions in kind may be covered by the EKN (machinery and in some cases patents and other industrial property). The guartantee covers the three main categories of political risk and applies both to the original investment and to distributed earnings of up to 8 per cent p.a. However, the total amount of distributed earnings must not exceed 24 per cent of the amount of the original investment. Reinvested profits are guaranteed on the condition that they were transferable at the time of reinvestment. In case of loss, compensation will amount to a maximum of 90 per cent and will normally not be less than 80 per cent of the insured capital. The maximum amount of coverage for a particular guarantee may be phased out according to a plan set out in the guarantee contract. Moreover, compensation will not take place before the investor has appropriately appealed to the local authorities. Normally, guarantees will be issued for a limited period, not exceeding 15 years. In exceptional cases, the period may be extended up to 20 years.

The fee for the three risks combined is 0.7 per cent p.a. of the current amount of coverage. If the guarantee also includes distributed earnings an additional lump sum premium will be charged. In exceptional cases, when not all types of risks are covered, lower premium rates will apply.

Fiscal Measures

In principle, both the tax rates on net income and depreciation allowances are the same for domestic and foreign operations. However, unless a double taxation treaty applies, foreign tax on foreign income may under certain conditions be deducted from gross profits as a cost or credited against Swedish state income tax.

To date, 21 agreements on the avoidance of double taxation have been signed with developing countries [Argentina, Bangladesh, Brazil, Egypt, India, Israel, Kenya, Korea (South), Liberia, Malaysia, Malta, Morocco, Pakistan, Peru, Philippines, Singapore, Sri Lanka, Thailand, Tunisia, Tanzania and Zambia]. Arrangements for the avoidance of double taxation have been made with Barbados, Botswana, Burundi, Cyprus, Ghana, Jamaica, Malawi, Mauritius, Nigeria, Rwanda, Seychelles and Sierra Leone.

As a general rule the tax treaties with developing countries provide for proportionally higher taxation in the host country than do tax agreements between Sweden and the industrialised countries. Under a treaty and also under the "exemption" method, a Swedish company will generally be exempt from domestic tax on dividends from a foreign subsidiary. On the other hand, if the "tax credit" method is used (as a general method or for certain types of income) Sweden has agreed to a credit for taxes spared in recognition of the incentives granted by the host country.

The Public Investment Corporation, SWEDFUND

The Swedish Fund for Industrial Co-operation with Developing Countries, SWEDFUND(2), which became operational in 1979, is an independent foundation with an authorised capital of S.Kr.100 million ($20 million). The Fund is allowed to borrow three times its paid-in capital with a government guarantee.

The purpose of the SWEDFUND is to promote the formation and development of industrial activities in developing countries mainly by:

a) acting as a broker between interested parties in developing countries and the Swedish business community;
b) financing, in part, feasibility studies; and
c) contributing with equity participation and/or loans and guarantees in joint ventures.

SWEDFUND's total contribution in the form of equity, loans and guarantees should normally not exceed 30 per cent of the total project costs.

The fund co-operates with public as well as co-operative and private partners of any size both in Sweden and in developing countries, but with particular emphasis on small and medium-sized firms. In particular, SWEDFUND

---

2. SWEDFUND, Jacobs Torg 3, S-10327 Stockholm, Box 16360, Telephone 08-231740, Telex 14135 Swefund S.

promotes projects in those countries which already have long-standing development co-operation relationships with Sweden or which pursue development policies consistent with the aims and targets established for the official Swedish development co-operation programme.

Only those projects are considered which have a favourable impact on the development of the host country and which have the approbation of the Government of that country. When assessing the economic impact of a project, SWEDFUND pays special attention to:

a) the creation of new job opportunities;
b) the training and development of manpower;
c) the transfer of technology and the adaptation of techniques to local conditions;
d) the foreign exchange effects;
e) the environmental impact;
f) the prospects of integration in the local economy and society.

Not only new ventures but also the expansion of existing enterprises may be considered. The exploitation of mineral and other natural resources are not eligible for SWEDFUND support unless they include an element of manufacturing. Contributions by the Fund are not conditional upon Swedish equipment being purchased for the project. Active local participation is usually a prerequisite for the Fund's participation. The local participants can be manufacturing companies, investment banks, development corporations or private individuals.

Although SWEDFUND is an independent body which makes its contributions to projects on the basis of its own analysis, it works closely with the Swedish International Development Authority (SIDA) concerning such matters as studies of industrial development plans and individual projects and with the National Swedish Board for Technical Development in matters such as the application of appropriate technology.

SWEDFUND does not, as a rule, participate in projects which have a debt/equity ratio of more than 65/35. When its equity participation is no longer required, the Fund may sell its shares to other project partners, preferably those of the host country. Shareholding is not a condition for the extension of loans by the Fund. Loans normally have a grace period corresponding to the construction and start up period of the project. Thereafter the loans are to be repaid over a period not exceeding ten years.

15. SWITZERLAND

Exchange Control

Outward direct investment is free.

Bilateral Investment Protection Agreements

Between 1961 and 1981, bilateral agreements for the promotion and protection of investments have been signed with 17 countries (Tunisia, Tanzania, Costa Rica, Honduras, Ecuador, South Korea, Uganda, Zaïre, Egypt, Indonesia, Sudan, Jordan, Syria, Malaysia, Singapore, Mali and Sri Lanka), agreements on commerce, investment protection and technical co-operation with 14 countries (Niger, Guinea, Ivory Coast, Senegal, Congo, Cameroon, Togo, Madagascar, Malta, Benin, Chad, Upper Volta, Gabon, Mauritania), agreements on commerce and investment protection with 2 countries (Rwanda, Central African Republic) and a friendship and commercial treaty including a clause on investment protection with Liberia. The main provisions of such bilateral agreements are as follows:

a) a guarantee of non-discrimination in the form of a national treatment clause and a most favoured nation clause;
b) a guarantee of the transfer of investment earnings, and of the repatriation of the initial capital when the investment is terminated;
c) a guarantee against arbitrary expropriation or nationalisation and a compensation clause providing for rapid, fair, and effective compensation of an investor who is directly or indirectly deprived of his assets;
d) arbitration procedures.

Investment Guarantee Scheme

The Swiss scheme for the guarantee of investments in developing countries against non-commercial risk, established in 1970, is administered by the Department of Economics in agreement with the Department of Politics and

Finance. The guarantee normally applies only to equity participation, but can be extended to foreign loans issued in Switzerland. Only new investments which promote the economic development of the recipient country can receive the guarantee. The limit for total government commitments under the guarantee has been fixed at Sw.Frs.500 million ($250 million). Investment coverage at the end of 1979 amounted to $40 million.

The guarantee covers the three main categories of political risk. In addition, for loan capital and interest it can be extended to cover insolvency or refusal to pay on the part of governments and other public authorities. In addition to new investment, the guarantee also applies to reinvested earnings. The guarantee of income on participation capital is limited to 24 per cent the latter for the entire duration of the guarantee. This guarantee covers investment risks up to a maximum of 70 per cent of the sum invested. The guarantee for equity capital is reduced by at least 5 per cent per annum of the initial capital guaranteed. The premium for coverage against non-commercial risks is 1.25 per cent p.a. of the current amount. The same percentage is applicable to loan capital for coverage against transfer risk and insolvency or refusal to pay, while for income on capital it is equal to 4 per cent of the anticipated annual income. For investments involving particularly large risks, the premium can be raised to as much as double. If certain risks are absent the rate can be reduced by an appropriate amount. If the government of the host country does not guarantee the repayment of funds due to the foreign investor, the premium is increased by 0.5 per cent of the amount of loan capital.

Fiscal Measures

There are no special tax advantages in Switzerland to promote direct investment in developing countries. The Confederation and the Cantons have formal agreements for the avoidance of double taxation of income with the following developing countries: Pakistan, Spain, Trinidad and Tobago, Portugal, Malaysia and Singapore.

16. UNITED KINGDOM

Exchange Control

Outward direct investment is free.

Bilateral Investment Protection Agreements

To date, the United Kingdom has 19 formal bilateral agreements with developing countries for the protection of foreign direct investment.

Investment Guarantee Scheme

The scheme, which came into operation in July 1972, is administered by the Export Credits Guarantee Department, ECGD(1) and applies to new investments in virtually all foreign countries. In principle, all companies carrying on business in the United Kingdom, or companies controlled by them are eligible for a guarantee except unincorporated branches of foreign companies and their subsidiaries used solely for the purpose of channelling investment funds.

To be eligible, the investment must be regarded as assisting in the development of the host country, and must be approved by that country. Cover is in principle available for eligible investment in any legally constituted foreign enterprise, including an unincorporated branch of the investor or a partnership, carrying on business in any country outside the United Kingdom.

The scheme provides coverage for equity and loan investments against the three principal categories of political risk (i.e. expropriation, war and restriction on remittances) and is primarily intended to cover those investments in which the investor has a management or trading interest. Cover is also available for portfolio investment provided that it represents at least 10 per

---

1. ECGD, Aldermanbury House, P.O. Box 272, London EC2P 2EL, Telephone: (1)606 6699; Telex: 883601.

cent of the total capital of the project and is not less than £50,000. As the scheme is designed to encourage lasting investment the investor must intend to maintain his equity investment for at least three years, whereas eligible loans must have a mean repayment period of not less than three years.

The maximum period of coverage is 15 years. Coverage can be given for the initial investment and for remitted and retained earnings, but in total not normally exceeding 200 per cent of the initial investment. In the event of loss, the claim payable will not exceed 90 per cent of the amount covered. The premium is 1.0 per cent p.a. of the amount currently at risk plus a commitment fee of 0.25 per cent on any additional amount which ECGD is committed to insure in future years.

ECGD is able to assume liabilities of up to £750 million ($1.5 billion). Total liabilities outstanding at the end of 1981 were $250 million.

Fiscal Measures

In general, the United Kingdom domestic fiscal system does not have any measure designed specifically to favour direct investment in developing countries. However, the United Kingdom has comprehensive double taxation agreements with 78 countries, including most of the Commonwealth and usually gives unilateral relief for taxes levied by non-agreement countries. Some of these agreements contain "matching credit" provisions which prevent pioneer industry tax relief offered to investors by developing countries being undermined by a corresponding increase in the United Kingdom tax liability.

A United Kingdom resident investing in an overseas company is generally liable to tax on the gross amount of the foreign dividend but credit is given for any foreign withholding tax. Moreover, where the United Kingdom investor is a corporation owning 10 per cent of the foreign company, relief is also given for the foreign tax charged on the profits out of which the dividend is paid. Where the foreign tax exceeds the United Kingdom tax on the dividend the excess is not allowed as relief against other profits. The situation for overseas branches is similar: the foreign tax charged on the branch profits is allowable as a credit against the United Kingdom tax on the same profits.

Under the imputation system of corporation tax introduced in 1973, a company resident in the United Kingdom pays corporation tax at a single rate (at present 52 per cent) on all its profits, whether distributed or not. When the company pays a dividend, it pays advance corporation tax of at present 3/7ths of the amount of the

dividend which it can set against its ultimate corporation tax liability. A United Kingdom resident sharehol-
der receives a tax credit equal to the amount of advance
corporation tax paid by the company in respect of his
dividend. This is included in his income for tax purposes, but is set off against his overall income tax
liability or paid to him if he is not liable to tax.

The Public Investment Corporation, CDC

     The Commonwealth Development Corporation, CDC(2),
set up in 1948 is the longest established of the
development corporations of its type. While responsible
to the Overseas Development Adminisration, the CDC has a
considerable degree of autonomy as a statutory corporation. The Minister appoints the Chairman and Members
of the Board which is responsible for CDC staff.

     Since 1975, CDC's investment policy has become more
closely harmonized with general United Kingdom aid
policy, in particular as concerns the poorer countries
and the emphasis on renewable natural resources. It
accordingly aims to make not less than half its new commitments in poorer developing countries and in renewable
natural resources projects. Investments take the form
of wholly owned and managed projects (where local partners are not available), equity participation alongside
others, debentures and loans, including loans to governments and statutory bodies. The CDC particularly
favours joint ventures with local entrepreneurs and
local capital. It attaches great importance to sound
management and is prepared to provide this where requested. Its investments may be made in any developing
country subject to Ministerial approval and are charac-
terised by diversity in both public and private sectors,
an important amount of technical and managerial assistance and concentration on countries where the private
capital sector is relatively weak. Except for economic
infrastructure the emphasis is on large agricultural and
medium-sized industrial projects. In the latter field
CDC has helped to establish a number of local development finance companies in order to reach the smaller
projects.

     The CDC has considerable investments in the renew-
able natural resources sector - agriculture, ranching
and forestry - together with allied processing plants
(46 per cent of total commitments). Technical, managerial, and financial assistance is given to plantations
and smallholder schemes growing bananas, cocoa, sugar
cane, rubber, palm oil, tea and tobacco. Over the

_____

     2. CDC, 33 Hill Street, London W1A 3AR, Telephone:
(1)629 8484; Telex: 21431.

years, the CDC has developed an original technique of assisting family smallholders through the establishment of "nucleus estates" which operate on commercial lines and around which out-growers are encouraged to settle. Such estates can in turn provide credit and technical assistance to farmers, process their crops and, ultimately, become the property of the smallholders through the purchase of the CDC's shares. The CDC is also heavily engaged in basic infrastructure (23 per cent), principally medium-sized investments in power and water. Housing finance companies (both mortgage financing institutions and housing estate development corporations) and development finance companies (where CDC investment is usually in association with local governments) account for 11 per cent and 8 per cent respectively of total commitments. The CDC also has commitments in industrial plants such as cement, textiles, and chemicals (10 per cent), transport and hotels (2 per cent). As to the geographic distribution of CDC's activities, about 40 per cent of total commitments were made in Africa, 18 per cent in Asia, 12 per cent in the Pacific Islands and 14 per cent in the Caribbean.

When a project has been successfully established, the CDC may dispose of its investments to local or international investors. The CDC has no share capital and operates on funds borrowed from the government and from other sources. Government advances to CDC are made at fixed rates of interest below current market rates and with a substantial concessionary element for renewable natural resources projects. Under the current legislation CDC's overall borrowing limit is at present set at £500 million of which up to £480 million may be borrowed from the government. At the end of December 1981, CDC's approved capital commitments totalled £596 million ($1 billion) of which £410 million had actually been invested.

Other Official Support

Official Development Assistance funds can be used to finance infrastructure needed for investment projects and to provide local development institutions with funds to contribute local capital to joint ventures involving private investment in partnership with local investors or public bodies of the host country. Support for these purposes is available on a government-to-government basis and a request is needed from the host country before the aid funds can be allocated.

The Overseas Development Administration can provide financial support for pre-investment studies by private investors in developing countries. This scheme reimburses half the cost of approved studies up to a limit of £50,000 which lead to a decision not to invest. Aid is available only in cases where the host country views the aproposed development favourably and is prepared to give it the necessary priority.

Under the official technical assistance programme provided by the United Kingdom, the services of experts and consultants can be requested by host countries for drawing up development plans which may include a role for overseas private investment. In co-operation with the Overseas Development Administration, United Kingdom industry provides many courses for trainees from developing countries.

17. UNITED STATES

Exchange Control

Outward direct investment by United States residents is free.

Bilateral Investment Protection Agreements

The United States has recently begun a programme to negotiate a series of bilateral investment treaties with selected developing countries. A draft treaty has been developed, based mainly on language drawn from United States Friendship, Commerce and Navigation treaties and other countries' existing bilateral investment agreements. Key elements of the United States draft include: national/MFN treatment for foreign investment; recognition of international law standards of expropriation and compensation; free transferability of capital, returns, compensation and other payments; and use of international arbitration procedures (normally the ICSID) for settlement of a specified range of host government-investor legal disputes. On 29th September, 1982 the first BIT was signed between the United States and Egypt. Negotiations on a BIT with Panama have been concluded and preliminary negotiations are underway or expected to begin shortly with several other interested developing countries. The United States has also completed 114 bilateral investment protection agreements with developing countries, which provide procedurally for the operations of the United States Overseas Private Investment Corporation (OPIC).

OPIC, the Overseas Private Investment Corporation

The Overseas Private Investment Corporation, OPIC(1), was established as an independent entity in 1971. While inheriting a large body of private investment activities from the Agency for International Development (AID), OPIC groups in one institution a range of

---

1. OPIC, 1129, 20th Street, N.W., Washington, D.C. 20527, Telephone: (202)6321804.

incentives which in other countries are normally divided between the Investment Guaranty Agency and the Public Development Finance Corporation. A major rationale underlying the creation of OPIC was the provision of businesslike management for the various incentive programmes. OPIC's tasks are to conduct the financing, insurance and reinsurance operations on a self-sustaining basis, taking into account the economic and financial soundness of projects. The Corporation must support only those projects which contribute to the economic and social development of the host country and are consistent with the United States balance of payments and employment objectives. The 1981 Congressional review of OPIC's basic authority raised the $1,000 GNP per capita restriction on OPIC's programmes to $2,950 in 1979 dollars, enabling OPIC programmes to operate freely in 17 countries where they had previously been restricted. Congress also recognised OPIC's role in furthering United States trade objectives by inclusion of a mandate to support development projects having positive United States trade benefits and enjoined OPIC from supporting investments subject to performance requirements which would reduce substantially the positive trade benefits likely to accrue to the United States from the investment. OPIC was also granted the authority to insure against damage arising from civil strife.

OPIC is governed by a joint private-public board of 15 directors. The Chairman is the Administrator of AID, ex officio, and the Vice Chairman is the United States Trade Representative. Eight directors come from the private sector and are appointed by the President of the United States with the advice and consent of the Senate. Four public officers represent the Departments of State, Treasury, Commerce and Labor. The President and Chief Executive Officer of OPIC comes from the private sector. In building up its own staff, OPIC has considerable flexibility to draw from both the private and public sectors. OPIC conducts its own operations overseas, but has access to the facilities of United States missions should the need arise.

a) Investment Insurance and Guarantee

United States experience with investment insurance is greater than that of any other industrialised country. Insurance against the political risk of currency inconvertibility was introduced in 1948. Other measures which have followed are insurance against the political risks of war, expropriation and civil strife as well as guarantees of private loans.

i) Investment Insurance Programme

Formerly known as the Specific Risk Guaranty Programme, the Investment Insurance Programme offers investors protection against loss due to the political risks of:

a) inconvertibility of capital and profits;
b) expropriation;
c) war, revolution and insurrection, and
d) civil strife.

OPIC also offers coverage against arbitrary drawdowns of letters of credit issued as bid, advance payment and performance guarantees on behalf of United State contractors. OPIC provides coverage for United States construction firms against payment disputes, in addition to the principal political risks enumerated above. Moreover, OPIC has developed comprehensive insurance coverage for investments in oil and gas exploration, development and production. Insurance is available for all forms of such investments including production sharing agreements, service contracts, risk contracts and traditional concessions. Another of OPIC's specialised services is the provision of political risk insurance and financing for United States investors involved in international leasing.

Insurance is issued for a maximum of 20 years for equity investments and for the term of the loan for debt investments. The fees can vary, but average about 0.3 per cent for convertibility coverage and 0.6 per cent for expropriation and war risks. For institutional lenders up to 100 per cent coverage is offered, for others up to 90 per cent of the initial investment. Retained earnings can be covered up to 180 per cent of the original investment. The insured investment can be made as cash, material or equipment, processes or techniques, services, loans, and in some cases, long-term supplier's credits. OPIC will only provide insurance on projects which represent new investments or expansions of existing investments, and which have received the approval of the local government.

As of 30th September, 1982, OPIC estimated its maximum potential liability to be approximately $3.5 billion. Since its inception, OPIC has endeavoured to keep its risks within manageable limits. For example, OPIC has an agreement with Lloyd's of London for reinsurance of about two-thirds of OPIC's expropriation losses within a certain country and aggregate limits. OPIC's insurance guidelines limit its exposure in any one country and any one category of risk at 10 per cent of total outstanding insurance.

ii) The Investment Loan Guaranty Programme

Formerly known as the Extended Risk Guaranty Programme, the Investment Loan Guaranty Programme was established in 1969 with a $750 million issuing authority. This programme is essentially a technique for tapping the vast resources of the United States private institutional capital market, e.g. banks and insurance companies. The programme offers lending institutions 100 per cent guarantees for both loan principal and interest against political and commercial risks. Loan guarantees are only available for credits provided by United States institutional and commercial lenders to eligible projects. Generally, OPIC requires United States management participation, a financial stake in the enterprise, etc.

The standard fee for the loan guarantee is 1.75 to 3.0 per cent per annum of the outstanding guaranteed amount. As of 30th September, 1981, $317.3 million of guarantees were outstanding.

b) Direct Financial Assistance to Private Investment

A "Direct Investment Fund" was established in 1969, with resources derived primarily from OPIC's subscribed capital, presently $50 million. The basic purpose of the Fund is to enable OPIC to take the initiative and facilitate private investor's decision-making when private financing for a project is unavailable on appropriate terms. Direct loan rates are close to long-term fixed rates available in commercial money markets. Although OPIC is not allowed equity participation, it does make loans in the form of convertible and profit participation notes which strengthen the equity basis of the project. Portions of some loans are sold to commercial banks with an OPIC payment guarantee, revolving the capital fund more quickly. All Direct Investment Fund loans went to small United States investors.

c) Investment Encouragement

As part of its overall financing programme, OPIC has broad authority in the area of investment encouragement through financial participation in the identification, assessment, survey and promotion of private investment in developing countries (primarily by small businesses) ranging from reconnaissance surveys to feasibility studies. OPIC has authority to help finance a significant percentage of local pre-investment costs of projects it especially wishes to promote, e.g. industrial development in particular regions.

OPIC also has a Business Management Education and

Manpower Training Program which seeks to facilitate technology transfer and provide manpower training. For example, OPIC supports a UNIDO programme which trains Investment Promotion officers from developing countries and a programme developed by the Fund for Multinational Management Education to provide instruction to ASEAN businessmen in the acquisition and use of United States technology.

AID, the Agency for International Development

a) The Bureau for Private Enterprise

The Bureau for Private Enterprise (PRE) was established within AID to promote economic growth and development through stimulation and expansion of private business enterprises. The Bureau assists host countries in creating a legal, regulatory and policy environment conducive to private business investmentment by providing assistance and to identify critical constraints in these areas and recommending changes to alleviate them. Within this context, the Bureau focuses on promoting the development of and providing loan financing and technical and managerial assistance to private indigenous business enterprises either directly or through financial institutions both in the host country and the United States. In accomplishing these tasks, the Bureau leverages relatively small amounts of public funds to attract greater amounts of private resources.

Because of its limited resource base, the Bureau initially is focusing its efforts on 12 selected countries and the Caribbean Basin. To each of these countries, the Bureau sends a Reconnaissance Mission, consisting of senior United States business executives in targeted fields, whose task is to: (1) assess the overall climate for investment identifying key legal, policy, and regulatory constraints to private investment; (2) analyse the functioning of the capital market system to determine its deficiencies; (3) examine vocational and management training needs; and (4) identify key opportunities for development-oriented investment, focusing on:

a) Agribusiness and other smalland medium-sized businesses;
b) Vocational/management training for employment;
c) Capital mobilising institutions;
d) Non-traditional export business development.

To provide assistance to these opportunities identified, PRE has announced loan finance programmes as follows:

1. Co-financing with commercial banks and other

financial institutions in "appropriate highly
developmental projects".
2. Capitalisation of privately-owned intermediate
financial institutions which serve the private
sector.
3. Direct investment in selected business enterprises (e.g. agribusiness) where replication by
other enterprises would facilitate private enterprise development in host countries.

These loans will be on terms and at rates that
demand financial viability and commercial competitive-
ness, and do not reward inefficiency or distort financial
resource allocations.

In addition, PRE has launched a cost-sharing, re-
fundable feasibility study financing programme for potential projects in which the Bureau may wish to invest
through its loan financing. To complement its loan programme, the Bureau also finances assistance to support
local private enterprise development, concentrating on:

   i) helping governments identify and remove
      policy, legal, regulatory, and other con-
      straints to investment to improve the climate
      for private business development;
  ii) building management and technical skills
      needed to operate businesses;
 iii) developing capital market financial institu-
      tions and structures.

Underlying all the Bureau's activities are the following principles: first, developmental criteria must
be met, directed toward achieving a better quality of
life for the poor majority; second, priority attention
will be focused on the agribusiness sector; and third,
the Bureau will emphasize the wide range of possibilities for United States business participation in strengthening developing nations through private investment
and through the transfer of technical skills, management
expertise and appropriate technology.

In some projects, AID will be a co-financier with a
private bank, the International Finance Corporation
(IFC) or other multilteral or bilateral agencies. The
Bureau for Private Enterprise is developing a close working relationship with the IFC, in particular concerning
capital market development and investment in target
countries.

b) Housing Investment Guarantees

The Housing Guarantee programme is designed to make
available to housing institutions in developing countries long-term financing from United States lenders for

housing programmes which give priority to the needs of
low-income families. In order to stimulate the required
investments, private United States investors are given
full protection by AID guarantees over the entire repayment period. The programme encourages home ownership by
families of modest resources, and also promotes the
development of housing finance institutions in developing countries capable of mobilising local financial
resources through savings promotion and secondary mortgage market operations. Under the programme, investors
are limited by law and administrative regulations as to
the maximum interest rates that they may charge. Moreover, the programme places limits on the cost of housing
units to be financed in each country assuring access to
families of modest income.

c) Direct Financial Assistance

    In addition to loans made directly to industrial
development, AID directs industrial financing through
private investment funds, generally established in the
central banks of the developing countries. These funds
are subsequently channelled to private enterprises
through a variety of financial intermediaries such as
commercial banks, development banks or "financieras" (in
Latin America). AID also provides funds to regional
development banks. For example, activities such as the
expansion of port facilities and assistance to development corporations benefit from AID loans to the
Caribbean Development Bank. AID has also loaned funds
to the Andean Development Corporation, which included
the financing of sub-loans to the private sector for the
creation, expansion, modernisation and rationalisation
of regional industrial projects.

    AID provides assistance to agri-business projects
through development banks and investment companies. AID
Loans have helped finance a variety of agri-business
operations in Central America, in particular export-
oriented industries (e.g. processing and canning of
foodstuffs, fertilizer manufacturing and the setting up
of supermarkets). AID provides dollar loans and technical assistance to small indigenous entrepreneurs in
Africa to expand their enterprises, and to obtain management capabilities. Programme loans and Commodity
Import Programmes financed by AID for balance of payments support generate local currency as local buyers
use host country currency to pay for dollar goods. A
portion of these funds may be utilised by the host
government to provide local currency loans to private
development banks or to purchase shares of stock in such
institutions.

Fiscal Measures

The United States employs the so-called "Tax Credit" method whereby a corporation includes dividends received from a foreign Subsidiary in its taxable income and the tax is computed at the ordinary rates applicable to corporations. The tax thus computed is then reduced by the amount of tax levied in the country where the foreign subsidiary is located. Under this approach, foreign taxes are treated as if they were paid to the United States, which simply reduces the taxes by the amount paid to the country where the income originates. United States tax laws, therefore, are limiting incentives for investment in developing countries: income earned in those countries is not treated more favourably than income earned elsewhere.

However, there are features of United States tax law which mitigate this effect of offsetting foreign tax incentives. First, foreign subsidiary profits are not generally subject to United States tax until repatriated. Thus, if profits are reinvested during the tax holiday period, they enjoy the full tax holiday benefits. To the extent that subsequent dividends are out of post tax holiday profits there is still no dilution of the benefit. Furthermore, the United States foreign tax credit is calculated on an "overall" basis, i.e., all foreign income and foreign taxes are averaged for computing the foreign tax credit limit. Therefore, even if dividends are paid currently out of tax holiday profits, the United States tax on these dividends may be partially or fully sheltered to the extent of dividends received from high tax countries.

Other Official Support

The United States' Government has taken various measures to encourage, organise and subsidise private groups which contribute to the transfer of technical and managerial skills to industry in developing countries. Such private groups include:

- The International Executive Service Corps (IESC), a private non-profit organisation directed and managed by a group of leading American Businessmen. Its purpose is to strengthen private business in developing countries on request through direct short-term assistance to management, for which a fee is paid to the IESC. The volunteer businessman serves without compensation except for expenses. IESC pays all its costs in the United States. Requests for management assistance from local businesses in developing countries have exceeded forecasts and the programme has received unforseen momentum and acceptance.

The IESC maintains a roster of over 6,000 experienced businessmen and women, most of which are retired.
- The Volunteers in International Technical Assistance (VITA), a private non-profit corporation, helps individuals and small businesses in developing countries solve practical technical and business problems through correspondence. There is no charge for the services.
- Partners of the Alliance, an organisation for establishing links between the business communities of Latin America and interested counterparts in the United States, is another organisation which has been conducting a successful programme under AID.

18. MULTILATERAL SCHEMES

This section describes a number of multilateral and international schemes and initiatives which are not sponsored by any one DAC Member country in particular, but in which DAC member governments or firms participate. The various institutions are designed to provide incentives or protection for overseas private investment from developed countries. Schemes of a public nature are sponsored by public multilateral institutions (United Nations, World Bank, etc.). The institutions discussed are not intended to substitute for the respective national schemes of incentives but rather to complement them and, in some cases, to provide machinery for co-operation between them.

1. Guarantee and Protection of Investments

A. International Centre for Settlement of Investment Disputes (ICSID)

In the past, a large number of bilateral treaties have been ratified, and more are in the process of negotiation, which have as their objective the stimulation of investments made by the nationals of one party within the territory of the other. Such agreements typically provide certain benefits to investors by the other treaty partner, and certain arrangements to protect their investments. However, these agreements do not normally provide mechanisms whereby the host government and the foreign investor can directly settle, on a basis of parity, any dispute that might arise between them in relation to the treaty, (except perhaps that the investor should resort to available local administrative or judicial procedures). Instead, most treaties contain an arbitration clause whereby the two governments can settle any dispute between them.

One of the principal purposes of the "Convention on the Settlement of Investment Disputes between States and Nationals of Other States" was the creation of a mechanism for settling disputes involving a government on the one side and a foreign private investor on the other.

The ICSID was thus created under the auspices of the
World Bank to encourage the growth of private foreign
investment by creating the possibility of settling such
disputes by conciliation or arbitration.

The Convention specifies the circumstances and
methods under which disputes may be submitted to the Centre and the form and effects of the resulting conciliation or arbitration proceedings. A growing number of
investment agreements include provisions to submit future
disputes to the Centre and a number of host countries
have adopted legislation providing for acceptance of the
Centre's jurisdiction.

The governing body of the Centre is its administrative council. It is composed of one representative of
each contracting State, normally the governor appointed
by the States to the World Bank, unless a specific desig-
nation is made. Its seat is established at the IBRD
headquarters. As of 1st August, 1981, the Convention on
the Settlement of Investment Disputes, had been signed by
85 States, 80 of which have completed ratification. As
Table 9 shows, membership is heaviest in Africa, while
few Latin American countries have joined. All industrialised Member countries of the OECD, except Canada,
are members of the ICSID (Australia being the only Member
which has not yet ratified the Convention).

Since the jurisdiction of the Centre is based on
consent, the most likely cases to come before the Centre
are disputes arising out of contractual arrangements
which include an ICSID arbitration or conciliation
clause. The Convention permits submission of existing
disputes in the absence of a previous ICSID arbitration
or conciliation clause. Such disputes will normally have
arisen in the context of relationships which date back to
pre-Convention days. In the absence of an obligation to
come to the Centre, the host States generally prefer to
seek a settlement with the home State of the investor.
The fact that there are only few cases before the Centre
is not considered as an indication that the Convention is
not serving a useful purpose, because the inclusion of an
effective arbitration clause in new investment arrangements may result in an actual reduction in the number of
disputes.

As of 30th June, 1981, eleven disputes had been submitted to ICSID. The first arbitration proceedings, instituted in 1972, concerned a dispute between Holiday
Inn, S.A., a Swiss company, Occidental Petroleum, a U.S
corporation and the Government of Morocco. The second
arbitration proceeding, Adriano Gardella SpA, an Italian
company, v. the Government of the Ivory Coast, was registered in 1974 and the Tribunal rendered its judgement in
1977. In 1974, requests for arbitration were registered
in connection with disputes between Alcoa Minerals of

Table 9

LIST OF COUNTRIES HAVING SIGNED AND RATIFIED THE
CONVENTION ON THE SETTLEMENT OF INVESTMENT DISPUTES
BETWEEN STATES AND NATIONALS OF OTHER STATES
(as of 1st August, 1981)

1. INDUSTRIALISED OECD MEMBER COUNTRIES

Australia(1)	Iceland	Norway
Austria	Ireland	Sweden
Belgium	Italy	Switzerland
Denmark	Japan	United Kingdom
Finland	Luxembourg	United States
France	Netherlands	
Germany	New Zealand	

2. DEVELOPING COUNTRIES (DAC LIST)

a) Europe

Cyprus	Greece	Yugoslavia

b) Africa

Benin	Guinea	Rwanda
Botswana	Ivory Coast	Senegal
Burundi	Kenya	Seychelles
Cameroon	Lesotho	Sierra Leone
Central African Rep.	Liberia	Somalia
Chad	Madagascar	Sudan
Comoros	Malawi	Swaziland
Congo, P.R.	Mali	Togo
Egypt	Mauritania	Tunisia
Ethiopia(1)	Mauritius	Uganda
Gabon	Morocco	Upper Volta
Gambia	Niger	Zaire
Ghana	Nigeria	Zambia

c) America

Barbados(1)	Jamaica	Trinidad & Tobago
Guyana	Paraguay	

d) Asia

Afghanistan	Korea, Rep.	Papua New Guinea
Bangladesh	Kuwait	Philippines
Indonesia	Malaysia	Saudi Arabia
Israel(1)	Nepal	Singapore
Jordan	Pakistan	Sri Lanka

e) Oceania

Fiji	Solomon Islands(1)	Western Samoa

3. OTHERS

Romania		

1. Signed but not yet ratified.

Jamaica, Inc., Kaiser Bauxite Company, Reynolds Jamaica Mines, Ltd. and Reynolds Metals Company, all United States nationals, and the Government of Jamaica. In the Alcoa case the Arbitral Tribunal issued in 1977 a procedural order noting the termination of the proceeding at the joint request of the parties. In the Kaiser case the Arbitral Tribunal issued a procedural order noting the termination of the proceeding in 1977 at the request of the claimant. In the Reynolds case the Centre received a request from the claimant for termination of the proceedings in 1977. The first arbitration case brought by a Government against a private party was registered in 1976. It concerned a dispute between the Government of Gabon and Société SERETE, S.A., a French corporation. In 1977 the Centre received a joint request of the parties for termination of the proceeding. During 1980, two cases were terminated by an award (Société Benvenuti and Bonfant versus the Government of the People's Republic of the Congo, and Guadeloupe Gas Products Corp. versus the Government of Nigeria). During 1981, two new cases were registered (AMCO Asia Corp. Pan American Development Ltd. and P.T. Amco Indonesia versus the Government of Indonesia and Klöckner Industrie Anlagen GmbH, Klöckner Belge S.A. and Klöckner Handelsmaatschappij B.V. versus the Government of Cameroon

The Centre has published a survey entitled "Investment Laws of the World"(1), dealing with national law and international agreements affecting foreign investment in developing countries on a country-by-country basis, compiling constitutional, legislative, regulatory and treaty materials. Its objectives are to assist States in comparing investment promotion instruments in various parts of the world and to familiarise potential investors with legal conditions in various countries.

B. Guarantees by private insurers

Commercial insurers (e.g. members of Lloyd's of London and the National Union Fire Insurance of New York)(2) insure investors' establishments abroad against political risk. Both existing and new investments can be insured even if they are not eligible for official guarantees.

Private insurance may be sought by an individual or a corporate body for any asset held abroad, whether it consists of participation in subsidiaries, assets held in outright ownership, loans or liabilities to third parties. The usual basis for coverage is the assets held, but this may be varied at the investor's request. This

---

1. Oceana Publications Inc., Dobbs Ferry, New York.
2. 70 Price Street, New York, N.Y. 10005.

insurance is based on the declared value of the assets to be insured, in principle their real value, as opposed to the transferred amount as is the case with official guarantees.

The duration of the guarantee contract is usually one year. It is renewable but not automatically so. In this event there may be a revaluation of the amount insured. The fraction covered is normally 90 per cent but may be as high as 100 per cent. The premium depends mainly on the country concerned, but also on the nature of the investment and the geographical spread of coverage given to a single insured party. Even though premiums for private contracts are generally much higher than for official contracts (between 1 - 5 per cent, depending on the type of goods, country, duration, etc.), private political risk insurance might be cheaper in the majority of cases. This is because companies are not obliged to accept the whole "package" as offered by public bodies, which insure the whole value of the contract, but only the portion that is at risk at a particular moment. In this way premiums can be kept to a minimum.

Guarantees cover loss or damage to insured property resulting directly from the following acts: confiscation, expropriation, nationalisation, seizure, appropriation, requisition, deliberate destruction of assets or of the title to ownership of them or any other act amounting to deprivation or resulting in total cessation of business.

C. Multilateral Investment Guarantee Schemes

From 1965 until the early 1970s, Member countries of the World Bank discussed the establishment of a multilateral guarantee scheme. On the basis of a report prepared by an OECD Group of Experts, several drafts of the "Articles of Agreement of the International Investment Insurance Agency" were prepared. Discussions of the proposal were suspended because it was not possible to obtain agreement on a number of major issues including the basis of financial participation, in particular by developing countries, and the voting arrangements. Given the fact that several of the more advanced developing countries have become exporters of direct investment capital to other developing countries, efforts to establish a multilateral scheme which would cover these investments have been renewed in 1981.

For several years the European Community has been engaged in a policy of promoting and protecting direct investments in developing countries. In the framework of the second ACP-EEC Convention (Lomé II) of 1979, the ACP countries agreed not to discriminate among investments originating in different EEC Member countries. Bilateral investment protection and promotion agreements between ACP and EEC countries serve as the starting point of reference (covered in Article 64 of the Convention and Joint Declaration). Similar principles are expressed in the co-operation agreement completed by the ASEAN and the EEC. Investment promotion clauses of a more general nature have been included in the co-operation agreements with Brazil and India. Similar clauses might be included in the future of the Euro-Arab Dialogue negotiations on a Convention on Reciprocal Promotion and Protection of Investments, which would apply to all the Member States of the EEC and the Arab League, are continuing.

2.   The International Finance Corporation (IFC)(3)

The IFC was established in 1956 as an affiliate of the World Bank. Its purpose is to further economic development by encouraging the growth of productive private enterprise in member countries, particularly in the less-developed areas, thus supplementing the activities of the IBRD. As a United Nations agency, the IFC is an independent legal entity with authorised capital of $650 million subscribed by 119 member countries (as of 30th June, 1981) and its own management and operating staff. Its President and Board of Directors (20 Directors representing the member countries) are the same as the World Bank's. The Corporation also has an advisory panel, a group of six prominent investment bankers from Europe, Japan and the United States, which meets once a year to discuss general policy issues. The IFC's resources are relatively large and allow considerable financial flexibility in its loan operations and its equity investments. In addition to its subscribed capital and accumulated earnings of $159 million, the Corporation is able to borrow, principally from the World Bank, for its lending operations up to four times its unimpaired subscribed capital and surplus. These resources are augmented by repayments to the Corporation of its own lending and sales of parts of its portfolio to participants.

As of 30th June, 1981, IFC held a portfolio of loans and equity investments of $1,647 million(4) in some 314 companies spread over 71 developing countries. During the 25 years of its existence, the Corporation has invested about $4,100 million in nearly 600 ventures with a total value of almost $18,500 million. In recent years greater emphasis has been placed on helping to develop energy resources and increasing the availability of

---

3. IFC Headquarters: 1818 H Street, N.W. Washington, D.C. 20433 U.S.A., Telephone (202) 4771234, Telex ITT 440098 Cable: CORINTFIN.
4. Of this, $1,374 million was in the form of loans and $273 million in equity investments.

foodstuffs, in particular by improving processing and storage facilities for a number of basic commodities. For the past four years, over 50 per cent of the enterprises to which IFC has provided technical and financial assistance were located in low-income countries.

Reflecting the changing needs of its member countries as well as the changing character of financial markets, the IFC is now providing more assistance to developing country enterprises and institutions gaining access to international capital markets, with public issues, loan syndications and other techniques.

It is the Corporation's policy not to assume managerial responsibilities. Accordingly, its equity investments do not normally exceed 15 to 20 per cent and are often much less in large projects. The IFC is not usually represented on the board of the companies in which it invests, except in the case of development finance institutions. The Corporation provides advice and know-how on technical and financial matters through its staff in liaison with its industrial partners.

The IFC has developed extensive relationships with international investment banks and financial institutions, which may either be associated directly in the original financing of projects or which may invest in IFC's own loans as participants. As regards the sectoral distribution of its investments, the IFC's portfolio reflects an emphasis on the industrial sector, in particular cement, steel, fertilizer and petrochemicals, pulp and paper. Agro industry, energy and minerals have become relatively more important in recent years along with tourism, services, development finance companies and capital market institutions. The number of ventures being undertaken by mid-1981 was geographically distributed as follows: Latin America and the Caribbean: 33 per cent; Asia: 26 per cent; Africa: 25 per cent; Europe and the Middle East: 16 per cent.

3. Investment Information and Investigation of Opportunities

While most of the multilateral development finance institutions are involved in pre-investment studies of interest to the private sector, the most active institutions in this field are the United Nations Development Programme (UNDP), the Inter-American Development Bank (IDB), and the United Nations Industrial Development Organisation (UNIDO).

The Special Fund of the UNDP has as one of its main tasks the financing of pre-investment and feasibility studies. Projects in the field of natural resources are a speciality. The studies are conducted either by the specialised agencies of the United Nations or by Consultants. UNDP studies relate to projects which may be the subject of either public, private or mixed investments. Reference should also be made to the Industry Co-operative Programme developed with the FAO and other UN agencies, in particular with the UNDP, which is a body linking the UN system with industry.

The purpose of the IDB pre-investment fund for Latin American integration is to identify and help promote projects offering a basis for multinational investments within the framework of Latin American economic integration. The Fund is used to study projects and programmes which may ultimately be financed with public, private national or foreign resources, as well as the Bank's resources. The Fund can finance pre-investment operations in the form of grants, advances with partial repayment or loans. Studies can be conducted and financed together with other institutions from the Latin American countries.

The purpose of UNIDO (United Nations Industrial Development Organisation), a branch of the United Nations located in Vienna, Austria is to promote and accelerate the industrialisation of the developing countries of the world with particular emphasis on the manufacturing sector. It has developed an increasingly varied set of programmes such as pre-investment surveys, industrial management training, formulation of industrial development plans, assistance to local institutions active in the field of industrialisation, dissemination of information and investment promotion meetings for officials and business representatives from both developing and developed countries. A number of these programmes contribute to the intensification and improvement of international private capital flows.

Table 10

DEVELOPING COUNTRIES AND TERRITORIES BY INCOME GROUP(a)

LICs: 61 Low-Income Countries(b)		MICs: 73 Middle-Income Countries	
* Afghanistan	* Maldives	Bahamas	Malta
Angola	* Mali	Bahrain	Martinique
* Bangladesh	Mauritania	Barbados	Mauritius
* Benin	Mayotte	Belize	Morocco
* Bhutan	Mozambique	Bermuda	Nauru
Bolivia	* Nepal	* Botswana	Netherlands Antilles
Burma	* Niger	Brunei	New Caledonia
* Burundi	Pakistan	Cameroon	Nicaragua
* Cape Verde	* Rwanda	Chile	Niue Island
* Central African Rep.	St. Helena	Colombia	Omen
* Chad	Sao Tome & Principe	Congo	Pacific Islands (U.S.)
* Comoros	Senegal	Cook Islands	Panama
Djibouti	Sierra Leone	Costa Rica	Papua New Guinea
Egypt	Solomon Islands (Br.)	Cuba	Paraguay
El Salvador	* Somalia	Cyprus	Peru
Equatorial Guinea	Sri Lanka	Dominican Republic	Philippines
Ethiopia	* Sudan	Falkland Islands	Polynesia, French
Gambia	* Tanzania	Fiji	Reunion
Ghana	Togo	Gibraltar	St. Pierre & Miquelon
* Guinea	Tokelau Islands	Guadeloupe	Seychelles
* Guinea-Bissau	Tonga	Guatemala	Surinam
* Haiti	Tuvalu	Guiana, French	Swaziland
Honduras	* Uganda	Guyana	Syria
India	* Upper Volta	Israel	Thailand
Kampuchea	Vanuatu	Ivory Coast	Trinidad & Tobago
Kenya	Viet Nam	Jamaica	Tunisia
* Laos	* Yemen	Jordan	Turkey
* Lesotho	* Yemen, Dem.	Kiribati	Uruguay
Liberia	Zaire	Lebanon	Wallis & Futuna
Madagascar	Zambia	Macao	* Western Samoa
* Malawi		Malaysia	West Indies(c)
			Zimbabwe

NICs: 11 Newly Industrialising Countries		OPEC: 13 Organisation of Petroleum Exporting Countries	
Argentina	Mexico	Algeria	Saudi Arabia
Brazil	Portugal	Ecuador	United Arab Emirates
Greece	Singapore	Gabon	Venezuela
Hong Kong	Spain	Indonesia (LIC)	
Korea, Rep.	Taiwan	Iran	
	Yugoslavia	Iraq	
		Kuwait	
		Libya	
		Nigeria (MIC)	
		Qatar	

* LLDC (31).

a) China P.R. is not included.
b) LICs include countries with 1980 GNP per capita under $600.
c) West Indies include Anguilla, Antigua, Cayman Islands, Dominica, Grenada, Monserrat, St. Kitts-Nevis, St. Lucia, St. Vincent, Turks and Caicos Islands, and the British Virgin Islands. St. Vincent and Turks and Caicos Islands are LICs but are grouped here together with the other West Indies MICs.

OECD SALES AGENTS
DÉPOSITAIRES DES PUBLICATIONS DE L'OCDE

ARGENTINA – ARGENTINE
Carlos Hirsch S.R.L., Florida 165, 4° Piso (Galería Guemes)
1333 BUENOS AIRES, Tel. 33.1787.2391 y 30.7122
AUSTRALIA – AUSTRALIE
Australia and New Zealand Book Company Pty, Ltd.,
10 Aquatic Drive, Frenchs Forest, N.S.W. 2086
P.O. Box 459, BROOKVALE, N.S.W. 2100
AUSTRIA – AUTRICHE
OECD Publications and Information Center
4 Simrockstrasse 5300 BONN. Tel. (0228) 21.60.45
Local Agent/Agent local :
Gerold and Co., Graben 31, WIEN 1. Tel. 52.22.35
BELGIUM – BELGIQUE
CCLS – LCLS
19, rue Plantin, 1070 BRUXELLES. Tel. 02.521.04.73
BRAZIL – BRÉSIL
Mestre Jou S.A., Rua Guaipa 518,
Caixa Postal 24090, 05089 SAO PAULO 10. Tel. 261.1920
Rua Senador Dantas 19 s/205-6, RIO DE JANEIRO GB.
Tel. 232.07.32
CANADA
Renouf Publishing Company Limited,
2182 St. Catherine Street West,
MONTRÉAL, Que. H3H 1M7. Tel. (514)937.3519
OTTAWA, Ont. K1P 5A6, 61 Sparks Street
DENMARK – DANEMARK
Munksgaard Export and Subscription Service
35, Nørre Søgade
DK 1370 KØBENHAVN K. Tel. +45.1.12.85.70
FINLAND – FINLANDE
Akateeminen Kirjakauppa
Keskuskatu 1, 00100 HELSINKI 10. Tel. 65.11.22
FRANCE
Bureau des Publications de l'OCDE,
2 rue André-Pascal, 75775 PARIS CEDEX 16. Tel. (1) 524.81.67
Principal correspondant :
13602 AIX-EN-PROVENCE : Librairie de l'Université.
Tel. 26.18.08
GERMANY – ALLEMAGNE
OECD Publications and Information Center
4 Simrockstrasse 5300 BONN Tel. (0228) 21.60.45
GREECE – GRÈCE
Librairie Kauffmann, 28 rue du Stade,
ATHÈNES 132. Tel. 322.21.60
HONG-KONG
Government Information Services,
Publications/Sales Section, Baskerville House,
2/F., 22 Ice House Street
ICELAND – ISLANDE
Snaebjörn Jönsson and Co., h.f.,
Hafnarstraeti 4 and 9, P.O.B. 1131, REYKJAVIK.
Tel. 13133/14281/11936
INDIA – INDE
Oxford Book and Stationery Co. :
NEW DELHI-1, Scindia House. Tel. 45896
CALCUTTA 700016, 17 Park Street. Tel. 240832
INDONESIA – INDONÉSIE
PDIN-LIPI, P.O. Box 3065/JKT., JAKARTA, Tel. 583467
IRELAND – IRLANDE
TDC Publishers – Library Suppliers
12 North Frederick Street, DUBLIN 1 Tel. 744835-749677
ITALY – ITALIE
Libreria Commissionaria Sansoni :
Via Lamarmora 45, 50121 FIRENZE. Tel. 579751/584468
Via Bartolini 29, 20155 MILANO. Tel. 365083
Sub-depositari :
Ugo Tassi
Via A. Farnese 28, 00192 ROMA. Tel. 310590
Editrice e Libreria Herder,
Piazza Montecitorio 120, 00186 ROMA. Tel. 6794628
Costantino Ercolano, Via Generale Orsini 46, 80132 NAPOLI. Tel.
405210
Libreria Hoepli, Via Hoepli 5, 20121 MILANO. Tel. 865446
Libreria Scientifica, Dott. Lucio de Biasio "Aeiou"
Via Meravigli 16, 20123 MILANO Tel. 807679
Libreria Zanichelli
Piazza Galvani 1/A, 40124 Bologna Tel. 237389
Libreria Lattes, Via Garibaldi 3, 10122 TORINO. Tel. 519274
La diffusione delle edizioni OCSE è inoltre assicurata dalle migliori
librerie nelle città più importanti.
JAPAN – JAPON
OECD Publications and Information Center,
Landic Akasaka Bldg., 2-3-4 Akasaka,
Minato-ku, TOKYO 107 Tel. 586.2016
KOREA – CORÉE
Pan Korea Book Corporation,
P.O. Box n° 101 Kwangwhamun, SÉOUL. Tel. 72.7369

LEBANON – LIBAN
Documenta Scientifica/Redico,
Edison Building, Bliss Street, P.O. Box 5641, BEIRUT.
Tel. 354429 – 344425
MALAYSIA – MALAISIE
and/et SINGAPORE - SINGAPOUR
University of Malaya Co-operative Bookshop Ltd.
P.O. Box 1127, Jalan Pantai Baru
KUALA LUMPUR. Tel. 51425, 54058, 54361
THE NETHERLANDS – PAYS-BAS
Staatsuitgeverij
Verzendboekhandel Chr. Plantijnstraat 1
Postbus 20014
2500 EA S-GRAVENHAGE. Tel. nr. 070.789911
Voor bestellingen: Tel. 070.789208
NEW ZEALAND – NOUVELLE-ZÉLANDE
Publications Section,
Government Printing Office Bookshops:
AUCKLAND: Retail Bookshop: 25 Rutland Street,
Mail Orders: 85 Beach Road, Private Bag C.P.O.
HAMILTON: Retail Ward Street,
Mail Orders, P.O. Box 857
WELLINGTON: Retail: Mulgrave Street (Head Office),
Cubacade World Trade Centre
Mail Orders: Private Bag
CHRISTCHURCH: Retail: 159 Hereford Street,
Mail Orders: Private Bag
DUNEDIN: Retail: Princes Street
Mail Order: P.O. Box 1104
NORWAY – NORVÈGE
J.G. TANUM A/S Karl Johansgate 43
P.O. Box 1177 Sentrum OSLO 1. Tel. (02) 80.12.60
PAKISTAN
Mirza Book Agency, 65 Shahrah Quaid-E-Azam, LAHORE 3.
Tel. 66839
PHILIPPINES
National Book Store, Inc.
Library Services Division, P.O. Box 1934, MANILA.
Tel. Nos. 49.43.06 to 09, 40.53.45, 49.45.12
PORTUGAL
Livraria Portugal, Rua do Carmo 70-74,
1117 LISBOA CODEX. Tel. 360582/3
SPAIN – ESPAGNE
Mundi-Prensa Libros, S.A.
Castelló 37, Apartado 1223, MADRID-1. Tel. 275.46.55
Libreria Bosch, Ronda Universidad 11, BARCELONA 7.
Tel. 317.53.08, 317.53.58
SWEDEN – SUÈDE
AB CE Fritzes Kungl Hovbokhandel,
Box 16 356, S 103 27 STH, Regeringsgatan 12,
DS STOCKHOLM. Tel. 08/23.89.00
SWITZERLAND – SUISSE
OECD Publications and Information Center
4 Simrockstrasse 5300 BONN. Tel. (0228) 21.60.45
Local Agents/Agents locaux
Librairie Payot, 6 rue Grenus, 1211 GENÈVE 11. Tel. 022.31.89.50
TAIWAN – FORMOSE
Good Faith Worldwide Int'l Co., Ltd.
9th floor, No. 118, Sec. 2
Chung Hsiao E. Road
TAIPEI. Tel. 391.7396/391.7397
THAILAND – THAILANDE
Suksit Siam Co., 1715 Rama IV Rd,
Samyan, BANGKOK 5. Tel. 2511630
TURKEY – TURQUIE
Kültur Yayinlari Is-Türk Ltd. Sti.
Atatürk Bulvari No : 77/B
KIZILAY/ANKARA. Tel. 17 02 66
Dolmabahce Cad. No : 29
BESIKTAS/ISTANBUL. Tel. 60 71 88
UNITED KINGDOM – ROYAUME-UNI
H.M. Stationery Office, P.O.B. 569,
LONDON SE1   9NH. Tel. 01.928.6977, Ext. 410 or
49 High Holborn, LONDON WC1V 6 HB (personal callers)
Branches at: EDINBURGH, BIRMINGHAM, BRISTOL,
MANCHESTER, BELFAST.
UNITED STATES OF AMERICA – ÉTATS-UNIS
OECD Publications and Information Center, Suite 1207,
1750 Pennsylvania Ave., N.W. WASHINGTON, D.C.20006 – 4582
Tel. (202) 724.1857
VENEZUELA
Libreria del Este, Avda. F. Miranda 52, Edificio Galipan,
CARACAS 106. Tel. 32.23.01/33.26.04/33.24.73
YUGOSLAVIA – YOUGOSLAVIE
Jugoslovenska Knjiga, Terazije 27, P.O.B. 36, BEOGRAD.
Tel. 621.992

Les commandes provenant de pays où l'OCDE n'a pas encore désigné de dépositaire peuvent être adressées à :
OCDE, Bureau des Publications, 2, rue André-Pascal, 75775 PARIS CEDEX 16.

Orders and inquiries from countries where sales agents have not yet been appointed may be sent to:
OECD, Publications Office, 2 rue André-Pascal, 75775 PARIS CEDEX 16.

65958-12-1982

OECD PUBLICATIONS, 2, rue André-Pascal, 75775 PARIS CEDEX 16 - No. 42445 1983
PRINTED IN FRANCE
(43 83 02 1) ISBN 92-64-12424-1